OUTCAST

THE UGLY 'TRUTH'

POETRY FOR ALL

Author: Daniel Washington
a.k.a W42275
a.k.a. W412126
a.k.a. W58979
Walpole, MA Prison System

The entrapment of a young black man.
Understand the struggle.

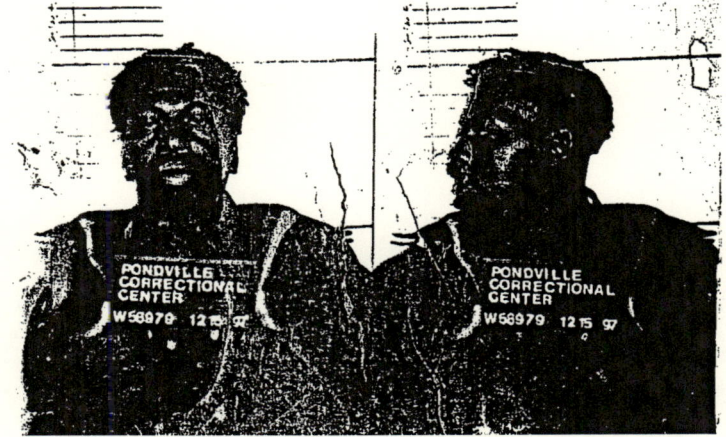

authorHOUSE®

AuthorHouse™
1663 Liberty Drive, Suite 200
Bloomington, IN 47403
www.authorhouse.com
Phone: 1-800-839-8640

First published by AuthorHouse 2/12/2009

ISBN: 978-1-4389-2494-6 (sc)

Printed in the United States of America
Bloomington, Indiana

This book is printed on acid-free paper.

OUTCAST THE UGLY TRUTH

U.S. leads the whole world
In it's numbers per prisoners capita
There are more black prisoners
In America than in South Africa
One in four black men in their 20's
Are in jail or under the
Control of the judicial system
The prison population has
Quadrupled in the last 20 years
Even though the crime rate had
Decreased by 26% since 1975
U.S. per capita spending on prisons
Has more than tripled in the last decade
We spend more on prisons than what we
Do on education
And the fastest growing employment
Is in prison guards
Joint fact, drugs increase your chance
Of going to jail
102% arrested in NYC
According to the National Institute
Of Justice study
Was uses of drugs
23.8% of all inmates admit to
Being under the influence of drugs
In Mass. the arrest for drug possession
Has increased between 1984 and 1989
Joint fact:
Violence and guns are destroying
Young peoples lives
The leading cause of death for black males
From ages 15 to 24 is murder
About 70% of youth in custody
Did not live with both parents
While growing up
More than half of the inmates in Mass.

Did not finish high school
Prison is a place where you
Lose all the things you took
For granted on the street
No women, no clubs, no privacy
No freedom, no respect
You can't speak your mind, write from
Your family can be take away and
Your own personal property is a
Few pairs of jeans and shirts
Cosmetics and a bunch of paperwork
Can be taken from you without warning
Prison practices are criminal in
Society and the law is just
Another human institute
7 days a week, three hundred and sixty-five days
A year. At 6:55 a.m. prisoners
Start their day off being counted
Like cattle and your name just becomes a number.
And these are some of the things
You would have to deal with
Being an outcast from society.

Free One Day

I took the bad that I had
And turned it around for the good
No more banging and slinging in the old neighborhood
No gangs, no drugs, no violence
To teach the youth to value life
No more silence, no more silence

I speak out about change
To some it's so so strange
How my life has been re-arranged
The misjudges, the pre-judges, the court judges
Some even hold grudges
When all I want to do is help
With a positive result

Each on teach one
Each one, reach one
No jails, institutions, no death
Liven in stress
You don't have to settle for less
I'll be the first to confess
I never knew what dreams was made of
Until I fell in love
With the hopes and dreams of being free one free one day
Shake my head and walk away
Beads of sweat run down my forehead
My adrenaline runs high; sometimes I wish I was dead
I grit my teeth in anger
I squeeze my fist tight
Where is my enemy
Who am I to fight?

My enemy is within me
A drug fiend
What does this mean?
Am I still a human being

Wait a minute

Maybe I'm a beast
That has no peace
That needs to be taught well
Caged in my jail cell
Made to live a life of hell
Why life got to be this way
Hoping and dreaming of being free one day
Free one day
Addiction
No one will listen
Your, caught up in a world of loneliness and despair
You're going know where
You're Life is so unfair
And you don't care
Because you get high, to get high, to get high, to get high
You need to come down
And turn your life around
Put down the drugs and walk away
Hoping and dreaming of being free one day

I stand in the crowd and not make a sound
But you hear me
My frustration is released
I come to you in peace
And you fear me
I talk about changed
And how my life has been rearranged
And you wonder how this could be
And as long as you focus negatively on me
Tell me
Are you free?

So I take a stand like a man
To teach the youth to value life
I speak from the heart with the love I got
And most times I even sacrifice
My experiences, in prison, on the streets, and in court
And all I ask, is for half, of your love, and support
Help us teach the youth, to live a better way
Than to be suffering, for nothing
Hoping and praying to be free one day, free one day

Watch the news, without having the blues
And something's wrong with your mind
Children are dying, from drinking and driving
And some are serving hard time
Young pregnancy, rape and robbery, and some just want to joy ride
Some are depressed and so full of stress
That they even commit suicide
So what do we do?
And who do we turn to
When personal pride shut our eyes
Do we bow our head, in remembrance of the dead?
Or help the ones who are still alive

Or do we look and ignore
The lives that need to be restored
As we joke, laugh, and play
Or do we lend a hand
And try to understand
Nothing good is going to come our way
Until the children are free one day, free one day

DEDICATION

I dedicate this book to:

God
My Mom, Dorothia Washington, who raised me
with wisdom and love even though we were poor, in
the projects, with pimps, hustlers and addicts.

Her and my late grandmother, Evelyn Johnson, known
as 'Ma Dear' who kept food on our kitchen table even
if they had to go fishing to provide, or scrape change
together for a bag of potatoes. They kept us alive.

I also dedicate this book to my loving wife,
Phyllis Washington who stuck by me in and out of
prison when I had no one else, she was there.

I also dedicate this book to our twelve children
who also understand what it's like to struggle
as a family and to still stick together.

To all of my friends and family and to those who
are still struggling day for day, we understand your
struggles. And down with the movement to make today
a good day and to make tomorrow a day of success.

To my big brother richard bubba washingtron
who died on dec 9th 2006.

To my dad who always was a hard worker and who has taught
me how to work and to use my working skills to make it in life
who taught me that no matter how menny times i fall to pull
your self up and to keep on trying to never give up nor give in.

Also dedicated to my late cousin Lamont Collins,
the Lewis family, the Johnson family and to all those
who have struggles with through my hardship.

This book of poems is about the struggles
and the plight of a young black man. His
perspective on life as it evolves around him.
It is a book for all to learn from, for most to relate to,
for some to understand and for many to wake up
and help to make this world a better place to
live for everyone.

D. Washington

the five Ws

there are five questions that solve crimes, if these
    questions are answered most cases are solved
America has been committing a crime against
    black people for decasteds
lawes have been made to hold us down, most young
    black men never graduate high school
nor make it to college.
in fact the only time a young black man feels as if he is
    graduating is when he is released from jail or prison.
so i am asking the same question that the judicial courts ask
    to solve a case and maybe we can have a understand on
    why these crimes have been and being committed against
    the young black men in America every day 'genocide

who? what? when? where? and why?

who?

who am i?
what am i?
were did i come from?

because of the hating separating, degrading and raping
because of the lichen, the tension, and all the other
    crimes i don't have enough paper to mention
we have know culture

who was the first man that sold me
was it the man that consoled me
or was it the man that told me
all babies are born free

kidnap a man and put him in chains
make him a slave and give a new name
then out of the blue he is set free
living in a world a refugee with know identity
because you murdered and separated all of his family
the American flag has been sown with the material of week wool
from the biggest lie
that all man are 'equal'
but who am i?

who?

What?

What would you think if i was to tell you that times have changed
    and that we are now all being treated equal as men in America

What would you think if i were to tell you by the year 2020
    that 95 percent of America would be people of color

What would you think if i were to tell you that the time is
    coming when the most popular language in America
    would be a language of another country like Spain

What would you think if i told you that i am a
    decendent of kings, there for i am royalty

What would you think if I was to tell you that with out my style of
    dress, music, talk, walk, slang, the way i sing, or do anything
That you wouldn't be 'what' you are
'Whatever that may be
Seeing that you slayed me and played me all through history
that now your children dream to be me
isn't it funny
the law of gravity, now reality
in a would that thought they possessed me
thought less of me
kept arresting me
laying stress on me
by depriving my family
brained washed me by telling me i am free
when all you did was changed the strategy
to keep me in captivity
piss in a cup?

Now i stand as a man with my chin lifted up
looking you in your eyes, trying to make you realize

that I am still a man...**what?**

When?

When did our children think that it was
    o.k? To disrespect their elders
Was it when daddy started buying drugs off of son?
Or when the 14-year-old girl was pregnant by every one
A child making a child, demanding respect
Think she is a women, because now she's
    getting her own welfare check
Or when grandma was know longer there to
    tell you how things used to be
How we use to unite with each other, and strengthen the family tree
Or was it when daddy was just hanging out at the bar
Hooking up his car
Wearing more gold then a movie star
Or was it when you realized that ma wasn't daddies only girl
He was once your hero,
And now he rocks your world
Rocks your world

I remember 'when' crack cocaine first hit the set
I saw some thing that i would never forget
It was a drug dealer's delight
A mothers fight,
And snitches was telling like it was alright

The police that was lazy
Started going crazy
And the jail houses was over crowded, over night

It made good girls turn bad
Bad girls get worst
feens want to go first
smoking all night all day
men turning gay
and department of social services
was taken children away

to some its there life
to others it sound strange
but this was when the whole world took a changed

when

'were'

were can one go
when you feel so low
and know one seems to understand your pain

were can you find refuge
in a game you always seem to lose
your sunshine always seem to turn to rain

were can you find peace
in your 'own' heart at lease
when its hard just to make your house a home

when people say they love you
then all they do is misjudge you
and once again you feel all alone

were is there justification
when life is just a bad situation
and some times you think you'll be better off with death

when times are so hard
you dear to pray to god
to take back his holy breath

were can you find a friend
who will stick in there to bitter in
when your broke in court and your child is in need of bail

or when your sitting in a cell
sick and trying to get well
and your only prayer is for a peace of mail

were can you go when you brought so low
when this wicked system is keeping you oppressed

you try to hold dear to a song or a prayer
but hard times keep coming bringing stress

were can you go
when a smile is what you show
but up side down its just a frowned
you try to hold on
you try to stay strong
but persecution comes
and knocks you down

were is there a place
when you show your face
racism and separatism
don't hold you back

were people don't hold know grudge
neither do they prejudge
and count you out because your black

'were'

'Why?'

Each time you threaten another black man or shall i say Nubian
brother in any kind of way, you send a message of violence,
of ignorance, of selfishness, hopelessness, and loneliness.
Knowing that you don't have know love for
him, leaves him in a state of mind
That I got to look out for myself, i got to do me per say
What does that do to us as a people?

As a people we are more interested in helping
     other people then helping our own
As a people we are more prompted to shed each
     others blood then to shed another's
As a people we are self destructing, and our own worst enemy.

Our brothers from other countries they don't
     want too much to do with us
Some say that the white man has tampered with
     our blood, that we are confused and lost
As a people we have know culture, we don't
     know our history, we are lazy
Don't want to work, UN healthy eaters, drug addicts, and theives
So those opinion put a UN natural affect on how others view us
As a people.

The fear of America is that one-day we may unite 'as a people
'Stand up and fight'
'As a people'
Make things all right
'As a people'
Then what would the world be like?
as a people
Haven't we've been 'hated' separated' and degraded' long enough
Is it too late to participate when times get tuff?
Why is it always our block that stays hot?
Surrounded by cops after dark
Why is it after we jump the broom?

We end up in the courtroom
Why is it that we feed poison to each other?
Then call each other 'brother
Why do we always want to fight and fuss?
And bight the Hans that feed us
down play our leaders
then be proud to be known as cheaters
Why would we rather dress like thugs, then put on a suit and tie
Think its fly to stay high, then cry, when one of
          our get high buddies dies 'why'?

Over one million men marched for peace
we could have tried to change at lease
But the death rate just increase
Why do we kill like beast?
'Why'?

Why is it that prisons are full of men like me?
when the rest of the world is living in Disney
And the only time i can find a job
Is when im am working in the prison yard

Why is my hood full of liquor stores?
Marianna on every corner, pimps and whores
Why all we want to do is look good and have a reputation
What ever happened to get a education
as we live in deep inflation
is there any participation
living in a unfear nation
we all we got
we all we got
why?

Contents

TAKE TIME OUT TO READ MY POEMS

The year is 1999
I'm at MCI Norfolk doing hard time
It's all psychological warfare
At the bottom of the barrel
In the middle of nowhere
Besides my Bible and my relationship with God
My TV is my only other true companion
Or me and my radio, walking the yard
I trust no one, and my associated are selected
And those I reject are just left rejected
One million personalities trapped behind these walls
Some have forever to do, and some are on their way home
Some aren't strong enough to make it, broken and all alone
Snitches, scinners and back biting, sell outs, also street gangs
Pimps, murderers, thugs and those with religious names
I vent my anger by pushing my pen
About the life I've lived, about the life I'm in
So read my poems with an open mind
And let's not forget those who are doing time
Cause it could be you or your child one day
Captured behind these walls and unable to get away
Please take these facts, investigate and make some changes
Cause the systems set up to treat us all like strangers
Don't believe that there is nothing you could do
To stop this mistreatment the choice is up to you
Some people say that some of us belong here
Now look at the life they live, hypocritical, psychological warfare
So many people say that my poems are too militant
That's just the life I've seen
The life I know

Continued

1

I found that I can express myself and my emotions
And share them with others when I write poems
I don't aim to bring harm to any one individual
By my racial and political facts
If I'm entitled to my opinion and what I say is not true
Than how come what I say makes you uncomfortable
Would you rather see me smile, wave my hands bye-bye
Stuff my feelings, live in phony ways, hide the truth and live a lie
Or would you rather know the truth so we can
     make changes in this world today
Or are you stuck on stupid and happy living this shameful way
Have you ever read my poems and truly got a
     handle on what was being said
The hurt, the pain, the suffering
The love and the life I lead
Here, read my poems, have understanding
Be blessed with wisdom and rich with knowledge
From the prisons to the streets, even teach my poems in college
I pray for one child's life to be changed, one life to be saved
One less mother shedding tears over another grave
One less prison cell to be filled, one less dope feen to be killed
One less war to be fought, one less thief to be caught
No less one less to be asked
Have you ever read my poems?
Whether your life is going good
Whether your life is going bad
Whether you're full of joy and happy
Or by yourself and sad
Take time out at work or at home
Take time out in a group or all alone
Take time out and read my poems.

D. Washington

Expecting Different Results...

On my journey miss directed

Having everything under control and neglected

Friends and Foes and those I don't know

Accepted and Rejected

Now I stand alone ... feeling the pain.

Friends and Foes can't remember my name.

Who got it good, is my sad song

Lonely only because my goods are gone

On my journey miss directed... used and confused

I lost the game once again.

Having everything under control, I set out to win but I lost again.

I can only blame myself and no one else

Doing the same thing over and over again...

Expecting Different Results...

D. Washington

Believe me
You will pay

The police was investigating the man for some time,
He was a crook, that took, advantage
Of young girls on the chat line
So the moral to the story is clear
When your lonely and in disappear
Read a book, take a nap, or say a prayer
See any tool that's misused can hurt you
Don't spend all your time online cause you
    don't have nothing else to do
And if you need friends
You don't have to meet them
On a chat line
And when you don't listen to your parents
And try to do things your own way
Everything has its price
And believe me, you will pay

And the door shall be open

My life has always been a constant struggle
Standing on shaky ground
There's always someone judging me
Taking my past and putting me down
Live and let live
Focus on your self
Stop hiding your faults by focusing on someone ells
A dog that will bring you a bone will carry one
If you listen to someone talk about the next man, and what he do
Then that same one won't have know problem talking about you
When you change the way you look at people
The people you look at will change
Change your Attitude
See one can find fault in any one
You will find what you seek after

You look for hate you'll find tears
You look for love peace and laughter

And the door shall be open unto you

I live in a world of constant stereotype
Were every thing is black
Were every thing is white
What difference does it make?
Its just the color of ones skin,
Dogs come in all different colors and there still dogs
Yet we can't just be men
Amongst men
Because of the color of our skin
Change your Attitude

And the door shall be open unto you

Spiritually dead
Living in darkness
Claming to have the light
Ignorance comes in all nationalities
In the world of stereotype
The man who sees his faults and refuses to correct them
Is a fool?
The wise man sees his faults and corrects them
With a godly attitude   and the door shall be open unto you

An exquisite delight for life

An Exquisite delight
The touch of your soft tender skin
The smell of your favorite perfume
The look in your soft brown eyes
The sound of your pleaser cry
An Exquisite delight tonight

Take me into your arms
Hold me on your breast
Let me feel your soul
Forever we were meant to be one
You're the best thing that has ever happened to me
For every moment that I have been lonely
I have been missing you

Your heart beat
Your inner pain
Your joy
Your sunshine
Your rain
Your smile
The way you stroke
For rich or for broke
The reason I live is you
Exquisitely for life

You are my soft breeze on a sweet spring day
You are my warmth in the wintertime
My gift from god and I praise him for making you all mine
And forever I shall hold on to my
Exquisite delight for life

And if one shall die, dear not cry
Dear not fret, dear not forget
All the wonderful years we spent
Loving each other, all day, and all night
Give thanks to god for giving one
An Exquisite delight for life

The touch of your soft tender skin
The smell of your favorite perfume
The look in your soft brown eyes
The sound of your pleaser cry
As you make love romantically to me, unselfishy
Tonight, for you shall be, for eternity, my exquisite delight for life

ALL ARE CALLED
FEW ARE CHOSEN

A man was down in a hole and he was trying to get out and he was yelling "help" "help" "somebody help me". "I'm stuck in this hole and I can't get out". Then came along a part time Christian, a lying hypocrite just walking along smoking a cigarette minding his own business when he heard the voice of the man in the hole yelling for help. He then looked down and said, "Hang on Buddy, I'll help you. I'm a Christian. I always help those who are in need. Why just this morning I gave two bums a dollar for a cup of coffee and last Sunday I gave the church $50. I believe that could be my calling, helping those in need. I have an appointment to go to and I'm late. When I get back I'll give you a hand but right now I have to go but I promise you I'll be back." Then he left. Then a self-righteous man walking by with his head held high looking down upon the man in the hole as he pleaded for help. The self-righteous man then said, "What in the world have you gotten yourself into. I never get myself into those kinds of jam. I taught myself to be smart. I'm not dummy like you are. I have a nice home, a good job and a new card. Nobody gave me any help. I worked hard for what I have. Nobody gave me anything for free. It's a dog eat dog world and you're on your own. I'm sorry. I can't help you." Then he walked away with pride. The man in the hole then said to himself, "That's OK. I'll just wait for my buddy to come back. He promised me he would (not knowing that the man was a lying hypocrite). Then one of those Christians came walking by, just as happy and singing (Just a Closer Walk with Thee) and then he stopped when he heard the man yelling for help. "Help, Help, I'm stuck in this hole and I can't get out. I've tried everything I can on my own and it seems as if the more I try the deeper I get into this hole. Can you please help me?" The Christian then without a second thought jumped down into that dirty, smelly, deep hole right along with the man. Then the man got very upset and said, "Now look what you have done? You got us both stuck in this mess. Now who in the world is going to get us out?" The Christian then took the man's hand and said, "Put your faith in the right place, let not your heart be troubled. I know the way out. I've been in this hole before. In fact, I've been in a lot of holes in my life and I've taken the same way out of all of them." The man then said, "How did you take the same way out of all those different holes?" The Christian then said, "Jesus. Jesus is the only way (John 14:6) and all we have to do is ask him and he is very present help in the time of trouble." (John 15:16) (Mark 11:24). Then the man said to the Christian, "Why did God take so long to send help?" The Christian said, "Our time is not God's time but God is always on time." The Christian then took the troubled man's hand and they started to pray. Before they even finished their prayer the troubled man was in a totally different frame of mind and Jesus set the captive free. "The Great Deliverer" From the lying hypocrite to the self-righteous man for the unbeliever.

ALL ARE CALLED
BUT FEW ARE CHOSEN

TITLE ???

Dogs shed and leave hair everywhere. Dogs eat their own vomit. Dogs move their bowels and don't care who is watching. Dogs bite and fight and kill. Remember the saying, "Like a dog in heat."

A dog in heat will hump your leg. A dog in heat will hump a telephone pole. Some people don't care who they go to bed with like dogs, and pigs.

A pig loves wallowing and living in dirt. Some folks like to keep dirt going. "Always in some sort of dirt".

Did you know that a snake can bite a pig and the pig won't die? But if you eat that poisoned meat you will die.

The snake, the crafty one, "Satan" feeds the pig some poison and you trust in that pig and believe those poison lies and eat up all he told you, and so you do, and so you die. Don't put your trust in man , put your trust in the Lord.

I don't care how good they say the dope is, its poison. And which one of you believes that he will gain something by putting his neighbor down.

The word of the most high, God is what you should live by. Don't put your trust in man's world, but in the word of God.

The word of God says we shall love our neighbor and the Lord with everything you've got. When the world sees us dong something wrong, in which we fall short of the glory of God. The first ting they say is, "I thought you were a Christian. Christian's don't do those things." My answer is, "If you knew about the Christian life, then you will be one."

Did you know that there are more words with 'do'
    in the Bible than the word 'don't'?
And if you do all that the Bible says then you
    won't have to worry about the don'ts.

DO NOT JUDGE

The name of this poem is "ME"
I am "ME"
And proud to be "ME", "A Black Man"

ME

"I'M" the first man
"I'M" in the image of my creator
I'M" a descent of kings so I stand as King
"I'M" a B.B.King so I entertain as a King
"I'M" a Rodney King, A Don King, so I conquer as a King
"I'M" a Martin Luther King so I preach as a King
"I'M" a King David, A Solomon, so I rule as a King
I am Me
So why would I want to perm my hair 'straight'?
So why would I want contacts just to change the color of my eyes?
That's not being me "I'M ME" just as I am
A descendent of kings, "The king of all kings"
The image of my creator
And the greatest creation of them all, it's "ME"
"I am me"
Lamb hair, hair like wool, big eyes, big lips, big shoulders, big legs
Strong arms and a strong back
"I'm me", I'm "black" created exactly in the image of my creator

I AM ME

There's style in my walk
The way I strut with rhythm
There's style in my talk
The way I strut with rhythm
Fashion designs have been made
By the way I style my clothes
And the way I strut with rhythm
It's a heavenly song I dance to
"Proud" to be "Me"
The way I strut with rhythm
So why would I want to be anyone other than "ME"?
When I am what I am – why?
Since I have been created
The enemy has invaded
Trying to kill my seed forever for sure
Because my seed is so holy, so blessed and so pure
Why am I such a threat?
To the international known beast
After all I've been created in the image of love
In the image of peace, generation after generation
Killing after killing, it's been a conspiracy
Why? Because I am what I am, and always will be.

A black man
And proud to be
"ME"

A WOMAN WILL LEAVE YOUR ASS

Looking into the mirror
A woman is a reflection of her man, that's what they say
Until I got married
I felt the same way
But I would never do to her, what she has done to me
And we got married under the misconception
That we were meant to be
We said our vows convincing
Till death did us apart
But when money got tight
And my wallet got light
That's when she broke my heart
The joy of having a family quickly went away
When she used my children
As a tool for money and wanted me to pay
I don't mind supporting my children
It's my responsibility
She took me to court
For child support and still don't visit me
I put her behind Cadillac's
Fur coats and diamond rings
But when I went to prison
That messed up everything
She blocks her telephone
So I can't call collect
Went out with sports coat
And bounced all of my checks
My mother tried to tell me
It's called mothers' intuition

Continued

But I was thinking with my little head
Too hard headed to listen
My dad was disappointed
He need not say no more
What he really meant with good intent
Was that she is nothing but a whore
But I got married anyways
Dreaming of a fantasy life
But reality awoke me
When she became my wife
Those nice little hellos
And those sweet good-byes
They went away like hair spray
And other cosmetic lies
Looking in the mirror
Our relationship was whack
What put the icing on the cake
Is when she got caught smoking crack
My children were taken away, awarded to the state
And now she finally writes to me, but now it's much too late
The disappointing news, she wanted to tell me
Is that she wants a divorce and she has HIV
A woman is a reflection of her man, that's what they say
Until I got married I too felt that way
I would never do to her
What she has done to me
Do good, she is there, do bad, she is gone
And that's reality
Take time out, look into that looking glass
Expect to only see yourself
Cause a woman will leave your ass.

D. Washington

IT'S NOT EASY BEING ME

Demons want to try me and deny me
Test the stress and then ride me
I always got to go that extra mile
Because you stereotype my style
I'm a genuine black man
On a spiritual level
Why you think we call you demons devil?
Cause you are slippery and slimy like a snake
You show no love and your smile is fake
The greed in your heart is for personal gain
To kill and make war in a righteous man's name
The things you have done and the things that you do
Is a prime and indecent, expression of you
As a man thinketh so is he
Like father like son, through history
Chain a man, hang a man, even lock him down
Work him, don't pay him, they lay him in the ground
Forever driven mad and viciously
And it's not easy to be me
Racism, separatism, hate crimes
From a mind of the demons
Money brackets, political tactics
From the mind of a schemer
From the White House Door
To the State House Floor
When can a black man have the key?
All in good time, what's on your mind?
Only for a political conspiracy
Racist demons, for those who don't know it
But your actions in life will always show it
They say times change but I can't see

Continued

And it's to easy to be me
You push me to check my attitude
And if I push back
I'm violent and rude
I don't' have a job and you won't hire me
Affirmative action forces your hand
To find a man from another country
And call him 'minority'
And it's not easy being me
All over the world
Throughout the nation
Stumbling blocks, trials and tribulation
I fight the demons, drugs and diseases
The devil trying to kill me
Have mercy Lord Jesus
There is something special
About the black man
One day we will fully understand
Why is the devil constantly trying to keep us oppressed?
Is it his vengeance on God?
Knowing we are blessed
Look at life today
Then study history
Then admit it to yourself
That you can see
The pressure, the reality
That it's not easy to be me
Demons want to try me, deny me
Test the stress and then ride me
I always got to go the extra mile
Because you stereotype my style
I'm a genuine black man
Caught up in a conspiracy
And it's not easy
No, it's not easy to be me.

WHY TALK ABOUT ME?

People talk about me
Because I got big lips
But I like who I am
Most black people got big lips
And I'm a black man
People talk about me
My hair is nappy
Nappy like hair of a lamb
That's the way I was born
And I like who I am
People talk about me
My skin is dark like coal
Like oil, like the rich dark earth
I've been this way since birth
And I like who I am
People talk about me
I look into the mirror
And my father I see
And some say my children
Also look like me
I love my family
And I like who I am.

Continued

So why would I want to be
Someone other than me
When "I" like who "I am"
Why talk about me?
When you talk about me
You talk about everyone on my family tree
Do yourself a favor
"Check your own history?

Look into the mirror
All of the dirt "you have done"
Then ask yourself
Am I God's son?

Generations down
Your goal in life
Was to make my life hard
And you don't even realize
That "I'm the child of God"

Just as I am
Without one plea
A black man, a holy man
And if I wasn't import
"THEN WHY TALK ABOUT ME"

I SHINE

I am a tree that cannot be cut down
I'm a stone which chipped off of a rock
Created on a mighty mountain
I'm a seed, planted on good ground
A waterfall springing from a holy fountain
I'm the son of mother earth
I'm the child of my heavenly father
I've been blessed since birth
And I'm gentle as an exotic flower
And like a bright and morning star
I shine.
I strike like lightning
And I can roar like thunder
With the power of a mighty rushing wind
And as pure as crystal
I shine.
I've been a king, the leader of mighty tribes
I've been a slave, the victim of being bribed
I've been perplexed, separated, hated, and segregated
And still like a rich piece of coal
I shine.

Continued

I've been s soldier in the constant battle called genocide
I've been a subject in politics where I've been paralyzed
I've lived in the way of many cultures and I survived
Laws have been made to hold me down
Many graves have been filled in the ground
I stand in crowds and not make a sound
And still I shine.
I've been called, hymie, pickaninie, negro, nigger
Afro-American, even been called black
I've been shut out, kicked out, without, bared out
And never welcomed back
And still like glitter in the eyes of a joyful child
I shine.
From the elements of the mother
To the characters of the father
From the joining of a brother
To the death of another
Even though I may suffer
I shine.
As long as the Lord is my Shepard
And I am of sound mind
This little light is gonna be alright
Cause I'm gonna let it shine.

THE HUMAN TOUCH

You can fight my wars, get right up there, on the front line
But don't touch me
I'll watch you play basketball
But don't you touch me
I'll watch you play football
But don't you touch me
I'll cheer you on, you can be my favorite player
But don't you touch me
I'll watch you fight, even call you champ, my champ, the people's champ
But don't you touch me
I'll eat your cooking, teach me how to cook that good old soul food
But don't you touch me
We can talk but you have to agree with me, don't you be too aggressive
We can look at each other, not too much eye
    contact, I'll listen to your music
But don't you touch me
Clean my house, wash my car, teach me how to dance
Shop at my store, give your money
But don't you ever touch me, without my consent
OK, I'll shake your hand, you have done a good job
But that's it, only a handshake
Don't pat me on the back, don't come around me after dark
You and your kind stay away, or I'll call the police, you understand

Continued

Stay away, don't move into my neighborhood,
    and most of all, don't you touch me
"News Flash" "News Flash" "Today's top story"
A young white male was struck by a car tonight
He lost a lot of blood and needed a blood transfusion
The hospitals only Afro-American doctor performed
An outstanding open heart operation
When the young white man awakened
He also agreed to the doctors professional performance
As the young white male sat there
With tears in his eyes
Not knowing that the blood donor was also black
....the black man's blood saved his life
Told the doctor that he had done a fine job
The doctor then said, "I could not have done it by myself"
"You also have a strong will to live"
The white male slowly put his head down
With a little smile on his face
And with a small gentle heart, he then said,

"THANK YOU, I'M TOUCHED"

Y-2-K- NIGGER BLUES

It Takes One To Know One

Nigger this, nigger that
When they gonna put nigger on baseball caps
Your mama never named you nigger
So why your boys call you that
No other race, at least to my face
Better not call me no nigger
It's a black thing, a figure of speech
That's what a young man wanted to preach
Nigger worker with nigger cotton sacks
Was once beat to death with nigger baseball bats
Chain 'em and hang 'em from the nigger tree
How to kill a nigger modern technology, the penitentiary
My brother – my brother "Why we call each other nigger?"
Sounding like the salve man with his finger on the trigger
Sound like the last word my great-grandfather heard
Before he was hung
I think it was "kill that nigger, kill that nigger"
We got one, we got one
One young man tried to preach
It's just a black thing, a figure of speech
Figure out where the word came from before you use it
Learn about the word before you abuse it
I read the Webster, Encyclopedia, Dictionary of
      the English language, the other day
And what I read just blew me away
The meaning of the word nigger
:A black person
:A member of a group of persons of disadvantaged social standing
"Second Class Citizens" "Second Class"

Continued

My brother – my brother, "Why we call each other nigger?"
You know we ain't no second class
Black people make up the largest racial and
    ethnic group of the United States
Blood, sweat and tears, worked the land for years
Made the foundation built to last
Nigger this, nigger that, nigger second class
When they gonna put nigger on baseball caps
Nigger t-shirts and nigger shoes
You can kill the nigger blues
In Y-2-K
From servant to slave
From nigger to negro, Afro-American colored people
In the next generation what they gonna call us then
Everything but neighbor, everything but friend
Why you call us that name
European slave traders ,political and social race haters
You're the one who should hang his head in shame
You got my black brothers killing each other not knowing
Where they're going, from where they came
I charge you, you're to blame
The one who should bare the blame, the one
    who should bare the nigger name
So I ask you brother, "Why we call each other nigger?"
When no one is greater, when no one is bigger

Continued

When we're all in the same melting pot
We're not the second class citizen
Don't call me nigger, I'm your brother so call me friend
Know the game, learn the rules, let's kill the nigger blues
Do it for the next generation coming after you
When your children call you one, then what you gonna do
Our moral respect for each other should be much higher
Let's not feed into the nation-wide trap of the universal liar
Stop giving a hand to the Klan who wants Y-2-K to mean you to kill
Let's rise together, build together, layback and chill
So the resolution for this year should be to know the game
Learn the rules and get out of the habit of misusing the word nigger
There's other words to use
We must prove to ourselves, our colleagues, that we're not the nigger
That they expect us to be
The choice is yours what vocabulary to use
You can say brother and be at peace with each other
And in Y-2-K you can kill the nigger blues
Your standards should be much higher
Your demands should be much bigger
Than to settle for less adding to this second class mess
Because it takes a nigger to call a nigger, a nigger.

WHO CARES?

Why is lie full of so much selfishness and hate?
Children dying all over the world
Because of greed, greed wants to dominate
Considering our differences, why can't we just get along?
Could you imagine if we all lived in peace
And there was no wrong
It gives us strength when we dream of better days
It makes us weak when we gaze upon another grave
How many times has one man taken a stand and tried to correct it
He stood, we listen, and then we rejected
Then later on we found that he was disrespected
He was right, but its too late, and now we regret it
Because we were lost
Malcom, Martin, Sallasie and the one we nail to the cross
Just to name a few
Who's gonna take the next man down
Who's gonna pull the trigger, you?
Mr. King yelled out in pain and he wasn't wrong
All he said while getting beat in the head is,
Can we all just get along?
How can you see the light when living in dark days
Racism, Torture, Death and other wicked ways
Stepping on heads to climb a ladder that's leading to nowhere
Who lives, who dies, who suffers, who cares.

WHEN GUNS GO OFF
WE ALL FEEL THE VIBRATIONS

He held a gun firmly in his hands
Gazing at the handle
then "BANG"
It just went off
He shot his best friend in the head
They rushed his best friend to the hospital
Family members and friends were crying and praying
Some were just sitting with a heart of pain, with no understanding
"I didn't mean it" he tried to explain. "It just went off".
The doctor came out to the lobby, with a tear running down his face
He said with a deep cracking voice, "He didn't make it"
He was just a little kid, he wasn't strong enough
"I'm sorry, he didn't make it" the doctor said sadly
The whole lobby broke down crying
Confusion and anger filled the room
"I'm sorry" he said, "It just went off"
He ended up in court on murder charges
"I'm only sixteen" he cried
"Man I didn't mean it" he said. "It just went off"
His family put their house up for bail and to pay the lawyer
The lawyer even tried to explain to the judge
"Your honor, the boy is only sixteen, with a future ahead of him"
"He hasn't even begun to live yet"
"I'm convinced that he didn't mean to shoot his best friend"
"I strongly believe that the gun went off"
The judge sentenced the boy to fifteen to life
"I didn't mean to do it" he cried
The jury that found him guilty wrote a little memo
On the bottom of the verdict
And the judge repeated to the young boy
"If you don't play with guns"
"They won't just go off"
"Guns just don't go off"

IT'S AMERICA'S
CRIME AND PUNISHMENT

There's a job to be done
For everyone
Loyal citizens fear not
For now is the time
To make up your mind
And face these problems we've got
I'm trying to remember
The crime I commited
I was so drunk and high, I forgot
The room was cool but the street was very hot
The task was difficult and the odds was against me
How can I fulfill my cravings, feed this money on my back
And remain free
It's a bad time of the day for money to come my way
And man this monkey is VERY GREEDY
Not in despair but to be whole and complete
To bring a better day for myself
As the monkey on my back started to attack
No dope, no coke, no wealth
And as good a friend he won't let me depend
On no one but myself
So I committed a crime, went to court and got time
America's solution – prison and pain

Continued

I didn't give no struggle
I didn't want no trouble
I just wanted more dope and cocaine
Is prison the solution
For my confusion
And burning desire for rocks
The court could have
Sent me to rehab
Or even a state detox
And now I must stay
Locked down this way
For a crime I don't remember, or no if I did
And within these walls
The tear drops fall
Going through withdrawals
Curled up like a little kid
Isn't that histatic
An unmanageable addict
The world's largest state convict
No methadone line
Or rehab time
IT'S PRISON
America's crime
America's punishment

RELIGIOUS PEOPLE OF THE COURTS
FOLLOWERS OF GOD

Love is unconditional, uncontrollable
Once you fall in love with someone
You will always love them
Love is blind, "God is love"
Even though we know that we are being wrongfully done
We don't allow ourselves to see the wrong
So we reason and use excuses for a logical explanation
Why we love the one we love
Love is addictive, "God is love"
Once you're strung out, you're strung out
Love is powerful, "God is love"
It can give life, change a life
And give someone a life worth living
Love is strict, "God is love"
We call it tough love
Sometime it is touch
To love, or to show tough love
Love is rich, "God is love"
One can have all the money in the world
But without love, one has nothing
Love is forgiving, "God is love"
Love holds no grudges
Has no vengeance
Is not resentful
Tells no tales
Fills no fails
Has no bails
Never fails
Religious people of the courts, so called *Followers of God*
If you love all mankind
Then what are all those men doing in prison? Following God?

UNCONSCIOUS ATTITUDES, WHY?

Unconscious attitudes
Unconscious and bias
Unconscious decisions being made every day
No trespassing, stay away, we don't want to pay
Identify the body
Stay or walk away
We are racially divided, yet co-dependent
This is my world, don't come in it
The federal bureau, America's hero
The world is occupied by men and beast
You and me, the human community
Racism, a human disease, unconscious and bias
Vote for the political liars
In a matter of time, we're going to be dead
Everyone waits for their Messiah
Let's sit, have supper, we all break bread
America goes to war, you saw it before
It's none of your business, bring in the troops, let's fight
Pick a man, call him holy, make him a saint
What kind of power do you really have, unconscious attitudes
Living in darkness, do we have the light?
A reconciliation between man and man,
    listen to what the preacher said
When the war is over, and the smoke is clear, I'm
    sorry the blood has already been shed
What is your profit? Sales from your own budget
The high tech work force of the future
Whose winning the battle on the war on drugs?
Who gets the profits, lock them down without
No equal access to nothing, no peace, no rights
Look at the man, with his hat in his hand
Sold dreams, given maybe's, unconscious decisions, no rights
Pollution illegal, legal prostitution, what's the solution

Continued

Who's shopping, did you get the gratification of the poster again
Keep your pistol in your holster, political extremist
"I'm innocent" she cried, and I understand, I understand
Unconscious decisions
Who does he think he is, making all of them kids
Five different women, not one wife
Now every day he's got to live this way
Take medication just to stay alive, for the rest of his life
Think before you act, think before you act (unconscious)
Can the appeals court overturn another conviction?
How can one hold a good conversation?
With someone who won't pay attention, unconscious
Dead rats and cool cats
No one's safe, no one's secure
How many times did he stomp on it?
He told me he got it pure, for sure
Identify the body, come on let's party, identify
    the body (UNCONCIOUS)
Racially divided, yet co-dependent
Man and beast, everyone wants a piece, you
    paint the picture and put me in it
A painted picture of the messiah breaking bread
American troops in double breasted suits
In a matter of time we're all going to be dead
You say it before, an unholy war
Civil rights fights and equal access to death
When the smoke is clear and the drugs are gone
Who won the war? Who walked away?
Racism, a human disease
And the world is a bloody mess, no less
Hate crimes and white lies
Unconscious and bias
Why?
So observant yet so rude
Watching man with his life in his hand
Thinking with an unconscious attitude.

THE STEREOTYPE

White journalist following stereotype
Who has all the elements to a compelling story?
Check the facts to the crimes in the community
Are they black on black? Black crimes
Can you understand the fear that white people have on black folks?
It's inconceivable that someone of that color can commit that crime
Read the rarity of the 911 tape
Is the identification clear? Is the identification clear?
The police are on the case, they would figure it out
Thinking like a loyal citizen
All available detectives respond
Who's playing into the stereotype?
Where are the Afro-American police officers?
What is the nature of the violence, fear, frustration?
In the turn of the twentieth century the racial tension
It's not safe to let our children out to play
The black community wants the same thing
    the white community wants
Stop and search the black man, stop and search
Who is going to answer the question for the panel in general?
Who disempowers the poor neighborhood?
It's not class, it's color, it's stereotype
Bad treatment and anger, the tragedy of stereotype

Continued

"No one never did nothing for me but put me in jail"
Said a young black man
What are the symptoms? Who's got the medication?
The disease, the disease is racism
Crime is up and unemployment is high
Prosecutors hit a blue wall of silence
So t hey send the Afro-American to jail
What's the big deal? Afro-American men go to jail all the time
Get the facts out of the community and onto the floor
"Blue wall silence"
Who is going to accept responsibility?
Damned if we do, damned if we don't
How do you look at the black community
"Stereotype" it's always about race

THE STEWART CASE 1989
THE EMIT TILL STORY
THE JOHN CROW LAW
WHY?
THE WILLIE BENNENT

LIFE IS SO UNFAIR

Shackled from the back I came
Woman in the black robe said my name
It was then when I saw the hateful looks
As the man in the grey suit opened his books
Another man in blue said he would defend me
He spoke of times and witnesses, murder and armed robbery
My mother was my witness, they said she was incompetent
Whether she can afford bail or not was irrelevant
So I stood with shackles on my hands and feet
Gazing out the windows, hungry for the streets.

I was never there, and I didn't rob that place
But since the man was like me, black with scars on his face
I didn't understand the legal terms and court words they used
All I understood was my lawyer saying if I fight, I would lose
Me being who I am, with the hate to lose a fight
So I confessed to this mess, by waving all my rights
Threw myself on the mercy of my new found friend
The lawyer, the judge, had me the young black hooligan
I'm too young to go to jail; I'm just a little kid
How can they put me away, upstate, to serve a life bid?
I didn't know what first degree, second degree or manslaughter meant
I didn't even know what homicide meant, I didn't, I didn't
I didn't do the crime, I cried, by then they said too late
I tried to appeal, from whatever jail, and
        hope to get another court date
Shackled from the back I came and shackled from
        the back I left, hoping along the way
And for another man's crime, I got time, and still locked up today
I'll never forget that evil room, the people nor the books
Their country suits and cowboy boots
Those rotten dirty crooks
Shackled from the back I came
Wit the hope of going free
They say the system works for sure
It never did work for me
What is in the heart of man, doesn't anybody care?
Forced to learn at a young age, that life is so unfair.

41

THE RIGHT TO REMAIN SILENT

A constitutional democracy, a way we'll never win
The north was singing when the saints go marching in
The south was singing Dixieland
Lincoln was singing the national anthem
And the Declaration of Independence
Was for what we all wanted: rights
Frederic Douglas was a great spokesman
Who worked with the underground railroad
With people like Harriet Tubman
Some slaves left the south looking for
The promised land, traveling days and nights
For what we all wanted
Rights
There's a new form of slavery
Prison, the long and lonely ride
Where some are victims of circumstances
But most are victims of genocide
I'm told I have high blood pressure
And high esteem, so they call me violent
With that they give me one right
The right to remain silent
Some speak with expressions

Continued

A frown with eyes of pride
But I speak out in writing
So I write in silence
My struggle in genocide.
Dark was always wicked
So I aim to see the light
After being told I was wrong for so long
I wonder, what's it like to be right?
Was Vernon Johnson right, by striking back?
Was Martin Luther King right, by being for peace and not attack?
We're the pilgrims, right? By transporting slaves
Was it right to kill a father
And make his children dig his grave
Is it right to kill nations, African and Indian tribes?
Either die or get drunk off the gin you used for bribes.
But I have the right to remain silent
What I say or do can be used against me in the court of law
I have the right to an attorney
If I can't afford one
You will appoint me one, from the court of law
Yah, right!
    You just want me to remain
    "silent"
    I GOT MY RIGHTS

MASSACHUSETTS CORRECTION INSTITUTION
MCI IS ROBBING YOU BLIND

If there was any corrections
In these institutions
Then why are there so many repeat offenders in confusion?
Prisons have always overflowed, even before the nineteenth century
They called it penance in the Catholic Church
Today they call it the penitentiary
Plymouth, MA, the Mayflower, Plymouth Rock,
    the Plymouth Slave Plantation
After the facts, Plymouth House of Corrections
    became the new warehouse slave station
In the late nineteen hundreds, the penitentiary
Modern day slavery, in-house industries
Population of mostly Puerto Ricans and Blacks
Filling the pockets of the Republicans and Democrats
Rivers of money flowing on a daily basis
Society is blind to what really goes on in these places
So I'm going to tell you some things about this supply and demand
To the best of my ability, and I hope you understand
You got to pay for everything, from head to toe
And there are a lot of things that society doesn't know
The Canteen Corporation, a billion dollar operation
The state doesn't give you anything, you
    don't pay for it, you don't get it
And when you do pay for it, no returns, they
    don't care if you can't fit in it
Everything from hair combs to toothpaste,
    with no mercy for the poor
Everything it takes for a human being to exist, they charge you for.
And all you tax payers and dedicated voters
    think we get these things for free

Haven't you heard, didn't you get the word?
Ain't no free gifts in the penitentiary
They took the speakers out of the TV's and
    make us pay for headphones
They got charge phones, overcharging us to call home
They also overcharge us for haircuts
Sometimes we get free coffee
But we got to pay for the cups
So when one goes to prison, who pays? The whole family?
The taxpayers? Or you, society?
What I would like to know is, where is all this money going?
In this land of milk, honey and money
Where the rivers are overflowing
They are robbing you blind, they are robbing you blind
We all are serving hard time, when they rob "you" blind
Who are we paying out debt to?
Who do we really owe?
Why does it cost our family so much money for us to be in prison?
Does society know?
TV, radio, hotpots, fans
And everything else is supply and demand
From deodorant, paper, toilet tissue, to peanut butter and bread
From shampoo, razor blades, to Advil and Sudafed
Just to name a few
They are robbing us blind
So, what can we do? Who can we turn to?
Because society is lost and brainwashed
And they don't think it's true
Don't say you don't know, because now you do
One day I hope you open your eyes
See the lies and realize
That you too, are being victimized
By the MCI's
MASSACHUSETTS CORRECTIONS INSTITUTIONS

MCI NORFOLK
MASTER CANTEEN LIST

CODE	DESCRIPTION	COST
100	KETCHUP	$1.09
101	TOMATO PASTE	$0.59
102	WHITE TUNA	$1.68
103	BAKED BEANS	$1.35
104		
105	FOLGERS COFFEE	$3.76
120	2lb. FLOUR	$1.01
122	ST.TOP STUFFING	$1.80
123	LG. HOT COCOA	$1.98
124	MIXED NUTS	$0.50
450	HAMBURGER	
451	CHICKEN	
452	ONIONS	
453	PEPPERS	
454	GARLIC	
455	FRUIT	
461	PANCAKE MIX	$1.34
462	PANCAKE SYRUP	$2.24
200	PEPSI	$0.60
201	DIET PEPSI	$0.60
202	GINGER ALE	$0.60
203	ROOT BEER	$0.60
204	MOUNTAIN DEW	$0.60
205	ORANGE SLICE	$0.60
206		
207	HAWAIIAN PUNCH	$0.60
208	ORANGE JUICE	$0.56
209	PK. GRAPEFRUIT	$0.55
210	APPLE JUICE	$0.55
211	INST. BREAKFAST	$1.93
212	CHERRY DR. MIX	$1.93
213	GRAPE DRINK MIX	$1.93
214	FR. PUNCH DR. MIX	$1.93
215	PEACH DRINK MIX	$1.93
216	LEMONADE DR. MIX	$1.93
217	ICE TEA DR. MIX	$1.93
218	COCOA	$0.15
219	CREAMER	$0.90
220	MAX. HS. COFFEE	$2.50
221	COLUMBIAN COFFE	$2.54
222	SUN-UP COFFEE	$2.08
223	DECAF COFFEE	$2.25
224	TEA BAGS	$0.90
225	SWEET & LOW	$1.09
226	SUGAR 2 lbs.	$1.30
227		
228	WATER (quart)	$0.41
229		
230		
231		
232	DECAF TEA BAGS	$1.75
233	V-8 JUICE	$0.73
240	S/F FRUIT PUNCH	$3.12
241	S/F CHERRY	$3.12
242	S/F PK. LEMONADE	$3.12

CODE	DESCRIPTION	COST
243	S/F GRAPE	$3.12
300	SNICKERS	$0.45
301	3 MUSKETEERS	$0.45
302	MILKEY WAY	$0.45
303	REESES P/B CUP	$0.45
304	HERSHEY PLAIN	$0.45
305	HERSHEY ALMOND	$0.45
306	CHUNKY	$0.45
307	KIT KAT	$0.45
308	M & M	$0.45
309	M & M PEANUT	$0.45
310	PEANUTS	$0.28
311	FIREBALLS	$0.50
312	SP/MINT LEAVES	$0.50
313	WATERMELON	$0.50
314	S/F HARD CANDY	$0.50
315	BUTTERSCOTCH	$0.50
316	STARLIGHT MINTS	$0.50
317	ROOTBEER BAR.	$0.50
318	DUPLEX COOKIES	$0.50
319	ANIMAL COOKIES	$0.50
320	SUGAR COOKIES	$0.50
321	VANILLA WAFERS	$0.50
322	STRAWBERRY CK.	$0.50
323	CHOCOLATE COOK	$0.50
324	P/B COOKIES	$0.50
325	CHIP AHOY	$2.66
326	ICED OATMEAL	$1.16
327	OREOS	$3.20
328	FIG NEWTONS	$1.23
329	HOT TAMALES	$0.50
330	CASHEWETTES	$0.50
331	AST. JOLLY RANCH	$0.66
332	TOOTSIE MIDGETS	$0.50
333		
334		
335		
400	SH. CHEESE SPR.	$1.64
401	JALEPENO CHEESE	$1.64
402		
403	GRATED CHEESE	$1.86
404	SWISS ROLLS	$1.03
405	CH. MOON PIES	$1.03
406	BROWNIES	$1.13
407	STRAW. SH.CAKE	$1.13
408	DEVIL CREAMS	$1.13
409	P/B CHEESE CRACK	$0.25
410	CH. & CH. CRACKER	$0.25
411	TOAST&P/B CRACK	$0.25
412	SLIM JIMS	$0.26
413	GRANOLA CH.CHIP	$0.25
414		
415	NUTTY BARS	$1.13
416	GRANOLA MACARO	$0.25
417		
418	CHOC.CUP CAKE	$1.13
419	COFFEE CAKE	$1.03
420	HONEY BUNS	$1.21
421	FUDGE ROUNDS	$0.84
422	BAN. MOON PIES	$1.03
423	BEEF JERKY	$1.09
424	PEP. BEEF JERKY	$1.09
425	OATMEAL CR.COOK	$1.03

CODE	DESCRIPTION	COST
426	LF STRAW.BOOST	$1.40
427	MARSH. SUPREME	$0.94
428	ZEBRA CAKE	$1.03
429	UNSALT SALTINES	$2.24
430	AP/CIN RICE CAKES	$1.60
431	CARAMEL RICE CK	$1.60
432		
433	DONUT STICKS	$1.13
434	SALTINES	$2.24
435	RITZ CRACKERS	$2.90
436	POP & CRUNCH	$0.88
437	WHEAT THINS	$2.71
438	CHEESE NIPS	$1.84
439		
463	SOY SAUCE	$2.06
464	CRISCO OIL	$2.40
500	WHITE BREAD	$0.75
502	WHEAT BREAD	$0.94
503	ENGLISH MUFFINS	$0.54
504	BLACK BEANS	$0.75
505	KIDNEY BEANS	$0.94
506	CHIC PEAS	$0.75
507	PINTO BEANS	$0.74
508	VEGGIE BEANS	$0.90
509	CORN	$0.88
510	CHILI	$1.55
511	BEEF STEW	$1.96
512	CORNED BEEF	$2.08
513	RED CLAM SAUCE	$2.05
514	WH. CLAM SAUCE	$2.05
515	RAVIOLI	$1.37
516	SPAGHETTI SAUCE	$1.36
517	TOMATO SAUCE	$0.85
518	CHUNK CHICKEN	$2.03
519	MUSHROOMS	$0.76
520	PICANTE SALSA	$1.55
521	SPAM	$2.63
522	VIENNA SAUSAGE	$0.80
523	JALEPENOS	$1.60
524	WHOLE CLAMS	$1.41
525	MACKERAL	$1.00
526	FISH STEAKS	$0.83
527	OCTOPUS	$1.90
528	SARDINES	$1.60
529	SHRIMP	$2.40
530	BROC/CH. RICE	$1.01
531	LIGHT TUNA	$0.95
532	MAYONAISE	$1.88
533	SUCCESS RICE	$1.82
534	FRIED RICE	$1.54
535	INSTANT OATMEAL	$2.19
536		
537		
538	HONEY	$1.07
539	HOT SAUCE	$0.73
540	IND. PICKLE	$0.50
541	PEANUT BUTTER	$2.00
542	FLUFF	$1.47
543	GRAPE JELLY	$1.70
544	STRAW. JELLY	$1.86
545	ELBOW MACARONI	$1.10
546	SPAGHETTI	$1.10
547	LINGUINI	$1.24

Foot Note:

There were a lot more underhanded things going on in the DOC that was not mentioned, like CO's working with criminal records, drinking on the job, staff stealing food, clothing and appliances, drugs and other illegal activities. Something must be done soon about these ugly crimes. If there are no corrections being made then things will only get worse with no corrections. If I leave in anger, I'm going to live in anger, and come back to prison an angry man.

Double jeopardy, look what you are teaching me in this institution. Are you part of the problem or the solution? People are dying in prison and you are never told. And if ever you do find out, the news is old. Now since you are aware of the problems, what's the solution to these ugly truths of the MASSACHUSETTS CORRECTION INSTITUTION.

HOUSED BY THE STATE

WITH NO SECTION EIGHT
THE HOUSE THEY BUILT AROUND ME

My house is full and dangerous
A place of steel and stone
Where everyone is a stranger
Overcrowded yet so alone
For one small crime
I got a lot of time
So I pace the floor day and night
And as I rage within this cage
I talk to myself to keep my head on tight
My home is hell
Is one small cell
That no other man wants to own
In here is death and despair
I live in fear in my only home
I wake up in shock within the dark
At the sound of metal keys and locks
The scrape of feet upon concrete
As guards march down the blocks
Homemade knives take human lives
No street corners hold more danger
And every day that comes my way
Each man remains a stranger
No one watches my back
In one second your life can be done
I don't want to kill, if I have to I will
And I can't trust no one

Continued

They dame today and took away
The man who lived next door
From peer pressure, loneliness and strife
He took his own life
He just couldn't take no more
It's been quiet upon my tier
Since death has taken its toll
Tomorrow he would be forgotten
Because life in here is cold
If something fatal comes my way
Or should someone take my life
Please tell my children I love them
And also tell my wife
That I'm blessed for all we shared
And all that they've done for me
And though I'm gone life goes on
Thank God I'm finally free
I did the best with what I had
And though it wasn't great
Do or die or suicide
House by the state
With no section eight
No house warming party
No champagne for nobody
No ribbons being cut
No Yo, What's Up?
Here's your brand new key
Just death and heartache, maybe a court date
In the house they build around me.

BLACK MAN IN THE PENITENTIARY
THE TRUTH SHALL SET THEE FREE

America – America
God shed His grace on thee
Through purple mountains majesty
Across the deep blue sea.

You told us we inferior, when we knew we were superior
Then why we in fear of ya
Unable to stop and stare at ya
"Prison", your so called rehabilitation
All across this mighty nation
"Black Man in the Penitentiary"
Held down by political chains, if only society
    can see, the financial gain
From your hypocritical games.
Supply and demand, for what is at hand,
    making the whole family pay
And after all, we can't even make a phone call without extra
Charges in the way, we can't express our frustration nor
Should we speak on discrimination, living
    on this modern day plantation
That they call rehabilitation
Great America, the land of the free
Laws have been made to keep us enslaved
Held down in captivity
Who is the victim and who is the criminal and
    why is our freedom forever denied
And if you believe there's racial equality
Then you are deceived and somebody lied
America – America, God shed his grace on thee
Through purple mountains majesty

Continued

Across the deep blue sea, Columbus discovered America
Like justice is true and fear, how can Columbus discover
America when the Indians were already here?
Is it history or his – story
Brainwashing society
If this is the land of milk and honey, then
    why is there so much poverty
"Black Man in the Penitentiary"
The truth shall set you free.
Black men played a major and unwilling and unrewarded role
In laying the economic foundation of the United States
Treated like animals, caged like apes, African
    slaves worked tobacco, rice,
Sugar and cotton plantations in the 18th century
And in the nineteen hundreds, "Black Man in the Penitentiary"
Resistance is automatic destruction
Broken spirits, lost in time, to sacrifice a man's life
Don't mean nothing
Immigration, an organization, divide and conquer, isolation.
Black Man in the Penitentiary
I heard through the grapevine it's OK to eat swine
And my worst enemy is my own kind
Somebody lied – somebody lied
My brother – my brother, we need each other
As we suffer through pain and deceit, they say no more
Civil Rights War, we won the battle, yet still got beat
We fought hand in hand, for this same land
We all shed blood, some even died
This is your land
This is my land
Then we made it home, poor and all alone
Locked up in prison cause somebody lied
America – America
Home of the brave, land of the free
Congress yelling racial equality

Continued

When prisons are filled over capacity, and plans are already in effect
To lock down the generation after me, stack the deck, stack the deck.
George Washington never chopped down no cherry tree,
And Paul Revere never rode no horse.
So did Columbus discover America?
Or did he come with a gun and take it by force?
Who is the victim and who is the criminal and why
    has our freedom always been denied
And if you believed there's racial equality then
    you are deceived and somebody lied,
Barbed wire fences, bricks and concrete
My body's in jail, my minds on the street, why
    does life have to be this way?
How can you judge me and tell me I'm wrong
When you break your own laws every single day
America – America, hypocritical land of the rich and home of the free
For those who don't abide, will be set aside, across the deep blue sea
Through financial gains and political games
"Economically"
Don't believe the lie that one has to die, to be truly free
Look within yourself, see riches and wealth,
"Black Man in the Penitentiary"
Live long and stay strong, educate yourself, stay in good health
Know who you are and stay strong, educate
    yourself, stay in good health
Know who you are and be all you can be and once
    you understand, my fellow black man
That God shed his grace on thee, through purple mountains majesty
Across the deep blue sea, for the "Black Man in the Penitentiary"
For we shall rise beyond the skies with love and unity
For God is in control
He holds the key to our soul and sets the captive free
So you stay strong cause life goes on
For the "Black Man in the Penitentiary".

LIFE ON THE INSIDE

I'm sitting in my jail cell
Dreaming about the streets
Nobody loves me
I haven't got a letter in weeks
As soon as I sit down and get comfortable, I hear the cops
Yelling out "count time"
I got to stand up for that bullshit and have a strong mind
Trapped behind a locked door
A bright light in a five by eight
Making peanut butter and jelly
To take the taste from the slop I hate
Sitting in the chow hall
In seats that are assigned
Tobacco and body odor
Eating with a crew of smelly creeps
Cops patting down bodies
Feeling on another mans' ass
The police crack a joke
An inmate just laughs
What happened to the convict
The standup man
Not the creampuff inmate
Folding on demand
Waiting on my property
Can't wait to get my TV
I paid two hundred dollars, after overcharging me
They took out my speakers, all I can do is see
Stole my remote control and they call me a thief
Mother fucking assholes
My clothes came in the mail
They said I had contraband
And I got to pay to send them out, I need some money
"GOD DAMN"
Another baby cockroach
Got stuck in my ear

The damn thing's eating something
Crunch, crunch is all I hear
My pillow's yellow and green
My wool blanket has never been washed
It's old and full of termites
And I can't keep them off
Today's laundry day
I sent my whites to get washed
Mother fuckers came back brown
Some more shit I can't get off
I make two dollars a week
All day I'm on my feet
Picking up cigarette butts
Man this sucks
Cigarettes cost $2.40
And I can't afford a pack
So I smoke rollies because they're cheaper
Man what's up with that
My fingers are changing color
From the nicotine
I can stop but I don't want to
Man, you know what I mean?
I go to an anger management group
But I ain't really upset
I'm just a lonely man on trazidone
Trying to forget
About what happened yesterday
I hope it don't happen today
I don't want to take medication
But I got to live this way
Every day I'm holding onto my mind
And pray not to lose it
The wheels turning in my head
And I don't want to abuse it
See it's all I got left
Besides my breath
Even that stinks
But I don't care what the next man thinks
Cause I got my crew
A bunch of suicide fools

Mother fuckers don't care about their own lives
Should they care about you
One man sets it off
And we all unite
Only three of us can read, no one can really spell
But we all can fight
There I stand in my new sneakers
My picture I.D. pinned to my chest
My hat on backwards
Sticking out from the rest
I'm so cool they record my phone calls
Give me brand new basketballs
Me and twenty men
Butt naked in a shower stall
Singing oldies but goodies
Like a think line between love and hate
Life on the inside waiting for a release date
The toilet paper is free
And I pay no rent
Surrounded by homos
Trying to get pregnant
But I ain't going out like no bitch
And I ain't running in fear like a snitch
God made me as a man with a dick
And I ain't going out like no faggot
Life on the inside ain't no game
Sometimes I look and say, "What a shame"
I went to the class board and got denied
I'll rap up before I make parole
But right now I'm just looking at four walls
But like a convict I hold on with pride
I'm sitting in a jail cell
Dreaming about the streets
Nobody loves me
And I haven't got a letter in weeks
I'm getting used to being denied
I thank God every day I survive
Because many die
From the hard life on the inside!

UPON MY RELEASE

Looking at my calendar
Watching my watch, tick-tock
As the years go by
Never pray for patient I'm told
But I want to go home "now"
I look in the mirror and I can see myself aging, aging
My God, where have all the years gone?
In the endless reaches of space
I gaze out of my window at the moon (tick-tock, tick-tock)
Thinking about the creating of the universe
The earth and the springs of the ocean
Surely there is a providence enlightening all of these wonders
Looking beyond my intellect, how long? How long? I ask
From the darkest space tones
To the high saparatones
I listen and I hear
And now in the vain unexpected experience
I now can understand the forty year Jubilee (my God, why?)
Look in the sky, fireworks ride high, and another year as come to pass
A lot of people have passed away
Children have become adults
And I'm still looking in this mirror (tick-tock)
I have no constellation, let me cry
I'm crucified with Christ, nevertheless, I live
As I pray for patience and live in exile, sin is ever before me
Daddy, what have you done? Come back in my life
My prophetic figure, you have changed humanity (I have aged)
What is your legacy, show me in the twinkling of an eye
Change the nations' history and leave me asking the question

Continued

How long? How long? I ask myself (tick-tock, tick-tock)
These walls are so high
These fences are everywhere
Everyday I'm walking on eggshells
Walking a tight rope
Don't cross the line and lose hope
The prize fighter could die
By stepping into the ring, don't fight back
Elect a pro-independent leader, somebody show me the way
No one wants a confrontation, we want to go home
In this isolated world, we are in every place,
       it's just another institution
Are you ready? Let me have your DNA I was told
Who am I? Where am I? Who are you? I ask
It's time, go home, it's time
So I just laid there with my eyes closed
Watching my soul leave my body
At life as the drug I used
From the darkness of space
Thinking about the creation of the universe
I'm free, I'm free with no place to go
Isolated in an incarcerated world
My God, how long? Why?
I have no constellation, let me cry, let me cry
(tick-tock, tick-tock) has come to pass another jubilee
And I'm still not free, there has been no peace upon my release.

OUT OF JAIL
AND OFF THE STREET

NO BAIL FOR A YOUNG HOOLIGAN

"Home" where I lay my head
Why can't you be satisfied girl
Just for the fact that I'm not dead
Give me a chance, I want to work
I'm going to get a job
I'm off the street, I'm at home
Girl, I just got out
You know times are hard
I'm not doing dope and I'm not selling coke
I'm fresh out of the penitentiary
Who's going to hire me
I'm used to hustling and having the finest things in life
Now what you want me to be
A scram, a minimum wage man, from nine to five
A Micky Dee's Clown, flipping burgers and shaking fries
"with my record" girl, you straight crazy
So what, I sleep all morning, but that don't mean I'm lazy
I just got out of jail, and the street is all I know
And now you are talking about putting me out
You know I don't have any place to go
But when I was hustling till dawn, flossing mad ice
Hooking you up on a daily basis, our relationship was nice

Continued

Now I'm trying to do the right thing
And you want to put me back on the streets
Screaming so I can benefit you
So you can show off to your peeps
I thought you loved me
I guess that was just another lie
You don't care if I got locked up 'forever'
Eat, go hungry, live or die
And who's going to take time to hire and train a young black male
A man has got to do what he got to, to survive
I really don't have time to fantasize, I realize
I realize I may have to take to the streets again
Cause when you right out of jail
There ain't no bail for a young hooligan.

"IT AIN'T NO FUN"
SO DON'T BE ONE

D. WASHINGTON

THE COMEBACK KID

How can a man get out of the can
And start using drugs again
There's no excuse for your foolish use
And you're going back to jail my friend
You can't find a job, create one
You want your own business, then make one
You don't know how, then go to school
Cause man getting high ain't cool
You can be a big willy, a big wheeler
A day to day small time drug dealer
If you're thinking about success and you think
Dealing drugs is where it's at
Then just turn around and cuff up
Cause you're going back
Ya! You and your boys making mad noise
Cap twisted back listening to gang star rap
And if you think that's where it's at
What you're thinking is whack
You might as well cuff up again my friend
Cause you are going back
Maybe you like being incarcerated
Outcast and separated
Undermined and manipulated
Misused and hated
Maybe you are institutionalized
And for you to come back ain't no surprise
Maybe you don't mind doing another bid
And those that know you
Will only know you as
The comeback kid.

D. Washington

60

REVOLUTION

From the playground to the prison yard
From the basketball court to superior court
From the play gun to the real one
From being a kid to having some
See life goes on by choices
Everyone wants to raise their voices
To give a brother bad advice
Like follow my lead, I got what you need, and
    this is how to make it in life
So, I used to be a stick up kid
Just to survive that's what I did
Ain't no shame in my game
I produce it and tell it
I can put it on the streets, raise the price and sell it
You know nobody loves me like me
And I love to love mentality
I used to hang out at the bar room after school
When the only thing we shot was pool
But today we won't go to shoot one another
Wave the peace sign and call each other Brother
It ain't over till the next man die
Take a stand and raise your voice, it's suicide
Some of us are waiting for a revolution
Until then they settle for prostitution
Selling one another short
Lost in this world with no support
Kids killing kids and children making babies
Blame it on the men for what's wrong with the ladies
Life is getting shorter by the bullet
The trigger wasn't made here so why we go to pull it
Liquor stores on every corner
Cocaine, heroin, marijuana
Barbed wire fences, bricks and concrete
A dead end street in a cop town
From the basketball court to superior court

We got no support until we're in the ground
So life goes on by choices
The world wants to shut up our voices
And no one can take a stand
You'll either stay poor and struggle
Or be a dead man
Once in awhile we get sellouts, who forget where they came from
Or even an Uncle Tom who believes he fought the system and won
So I turned into a stick up kid
In grammar school you taught me,
In the history books you forgot me
You told me about George Washington but
      not the Booker Tee's or the
Frederick Douglases and the ones that hung from trees.
Yah, Paul Revere road a horse
So did Columbus discover America or take it by force
No you claim not to be the anti-Christ
After stealing, lying and lynching all your life
It's just not human, it's unreal
Do you have a conscience, a soul, can you feel?
You've been a cold hearted murdered from day one
Hitler had the gas chamber, you've got the gun
You came to my land and stole me
Raped my mother and ran
Made my father work for free
Now we're coming up again
So put that down in history
You're more afraid of me than I am of you
When all the black me unite, then what are you going to do
You'll probably get crazy and go to war
I think that's what the nuclear bomb was built for
You'd rather kill the whole planet than to see me take control
So afraid that I'll treat you like you did me, you asshole
So take the young black generation and give them guns
Give them drugs and let the die, one by one
Or let them go mad and kill
So you can give them probation and lock

Them up at will
If you can get enough of them, you can stop the blood line
Out of sight, out of our way, and out of mind
So brothers let's make choices for changes in our life
No more killing, no more drugs, no more bad advice
See the only reason we should die is by old age
Not by another black man in a rage
We already got the weight of the world on our backs
Stereotyped, pushed down, locked up, short changed
Just because we're black
If I don't get any support from my own kind
Since life is made of choice, I'll make mine
All the judges in court must realize
A man is gonna do what he got to survive
This system is corrupt and so are the people who made it
Your law if flaw and I hate it
From the playground to the prison yard
From heart of greed to your faith in God
From the lies in history and the ones straight from your mouth
In grammar school you taught me,
In the history books you forgot me
You told me about George Washington but
    not the Booker Tee's or the
Frederick Douglases and the ones that hung from trees.
Yah, Paul Revere road a horse
So did Columbus discover America or take it by force
No you claim not to be the anti-Christ
After stealing, lying and lynching all your life
It's just not human, it's unreal
Do you have a conscience, a soul, can you feel?
You've been a cold hearted murdered from day one
Hitler had the gas chamber, you've got the gun
You came to my land and stole me
Raped my mother and ran
Made my father work for free
Now we're coming up again
So put that down in history

You're more afraid of me than I am of you
When all the black me unite, then what are you going to do
You'll probably get crazy and go to war
I think that's what the nuclear bomb was built for
You'd rather kill the whole planet than to see me take control
So afraid that I'll treat you like you did me, you asshole
So take the young black generation and give them guns
Give them drugs and let the die, one by one
Or let them go mad and kill
So you can give them probation and lock
Them up at will
If you can get enough of them, you can stop the blood line
Out of sight, out of our way, and out of mind
So brothers let's make choices for changes in our life
No more killing, no more drugs, no more bad advice
See the only reason we should die is by old age
Not by another black man in a rage
We already got the weight of the world on our backs
Stereotyped, pushed down, locked up, short changed
Just because we're black
If I don't get any support from my own kind
Since life is made of choice, I'll make mine
All the judges in court must realize
A man is gonna do what he got to survive
This system is corrupt and so are the people who made it
Your law if flaw and I hate it
From the playground to the prison yard
From heart of greed to your faith in God
From the lies in history and the ones straight from your mouth
From the statue of Jesus to the one called liberty
My seed shall go on forever, and forever I will be
As long as life is made of choices
To every problem there's a solution
Watch out, Demon of Power
There will be, a revolution, there will be a revolution.

WHO WE GONNA TURN TO BROTHER

Political action and affirmative action
Genocide is what we're going to one another
And forever more, we're killing each other
Sell out, Uncle Tom, house nigger
Master say shoot and you can't wait to pull the trigger
The jail house is full of brothers doing time
And the graveyard is overloaded from black on black crime
Fellas out snitching for a personal gain
Some are truly guilty and some have been framed
Some are selling out to climb the corporate ladder
We can blame the white man but it really doesn't matter
Cause we're killing one another anyways
Guns, drugs, dirty needles and AIDS
From high school dreams to political scheme
From the church hall to the city hall
He who represents himself has a fool for a client
And an independent man is not reliant
In a world of the rich, getting richer, the poor
     one day away from poverty
I stand in battle from all four sides
Stabbed in the back by black, and the white got me paralyzed
You don't have to be black to be a nigger
Ignorance comes in all nationalities
If we're all equivalent then why kill one another in greed
Living in hell, looking to heaven
Dreaming to escape to another place
Cause the world was built on blood shed
Killing for the cheese in a rat race
I'm unarmed in danger and I can't hide
I'm a target in a battle of genocide

Continued

Republicans, Democrats, Whites and Blacks
Lawyers, judges, police and crooks
Some steal from the state and some snatch pocketbooks
Some flip papers from a sky scraper
Some making pay from the alleyway
Some may struggle on welfare
Some are getting high and don't care
Some are in suits and some in rags
But the worst harm is from the Tom in a badge
Cause he goes out of his way to make my life hard
And the first thing he says is "I'm just going my job"
But in reality he arrests me to impress his boss
Like sell out, an Uncle Tom, a house nigger, he's lost
Who we gonna turn to brother, the man on the corner dealing rock
Who will shoot you cause you're on 'his' block
Or the man that didn't grow up in the ghetto
His skin is black but he don't know yo!
And some will just kill out of pride
It's nothing personal, it's genocide
It's time to come together
Cause we're all we got
And if we don't take a stand we'll fall apart
The jail house is full of brothers doing time
And the graveyard is overloaded form black on black crime
It's genocide and the only way to win the fight
Is to silence the violence and unite
Cause if we keep on killing one another
Then who we gonna turn to *"Brother"*
Who we gonna turn to brother?

FLICK THE SWITCH, THE POWER IS ON (Intro)

There are too many obstacles that keep us divided
And it's sad to even say
That to many; of us are brainwashed, rocked
    to sleep and too blind to see
The things that keep us mentally, spiritually and socially divided
We can band together at times when the going is good
We can stand together at times when we think we're safe
But when the fireman starts to spray us with the water hose
Or the dog trainer puts the K-9 on us
It's every man for himself
Someone once told me that that's what it's all about
"it's all about self"
While we all suffer, our mothers and children suffer
Because of this division
Divided and left standing alone
And here we are, so quick to fight each other
Over small mattes that can easily be resolved
Over things like a basketball game
"it's my turn on the telephone" and etc
Calling each other out of there name
"man don't disrespect me"
While we are being disrespected in other areas every single day
In many different ways
But our focus is on the wrong issues
And it's blinding
Too blind to see, why our family got to pay so much for
That phone call? For that TV?
What's all of this supply and demand jumping off about
Like crabs in a barrel constantly pulling each other down
Back biting and screaming with jealousy and strife
Misjudging and prejudging each other in negative ways

Continued

Judging each other by the style of sneakers we wear
Judging each other by the way we braid or cut our hair
Judging each other by how much canteen we get
Who got what and what's he doing time for
Instead of putting each other down
Let's start pulling each other up
By being persistent to assist each other
Do you have any sneakers? If not, how can I hope you get some?
Let's go to the library and work on our cases together
Let's figure out some way we can get out of this mess "together"
Let's stop living in darkness
Flick the switch, unite and turn on some power
So we can all get a grasp of things
So we can all see the light
So our families won't be so distant
So we won't be so isolated, segregated and separated
Flick the switch and let's start fighting this wicked
And cruel world together to make things right
Instead of getting shot down by our own peers
We been apart for far too long
It would be nice to get black together again
We can't win the game if the game is fixed against us
We need team work
How many times, just this year alone
Have you seen brothers get locked down for fighting each other
If we use our head, we wouldn't be fighting "at all"
We don't fight against flesh and blood
But against principalities, against powers
Against spiritual wickedness in high places
Against the rulers of darkness of this age
So let's unite, flick the switch, turn on some light
Choose to unite, in positive ways
United we stand, divided we fall
All for one and one for all, wake up, see the light
And you will be amazed
And that's why I wrote what you are about to read.

FLICK THE SWITCH, THE POWER IS ON

Oh happy days, oh happy days
When the saints go marching in
Most will be surprised, it'll be too late once they realize
"My God" it has been, a world wide
Revolution
When we unite and come together as one
The world will stop and stare
Some will stand in pride with nothing to hide
Some will commit suicide, and those who live, will live in fear
Behold how good and pleasant it is
For brothers to dwell in unity
Numbers is power, knowledge is power
Divide and conquer has been a successful strategy
So we need to come together in peace and unity
We have been divided for far too long
(flick the switch, the power is on)
It's time to come together and stand strong
Too much blood shed, too much wrong
The wickedness of the world is on our shoulders
The look of frustration on my brother face
Let's come together as one, my brothers
And heal the open wounds
That has infected our race
A house that is divided can never stand
We will either stand together strong
Or build our house in the sand
You might be saying to yourself
What I'm talking about won't change nothing
If you are, then you are the one to blame
For our violent, self destruction (flick the switch, the power is on)
It's time to come together with no more hesitation
No only for ourselves but for the next generation

Continued

Why are we so quick to shed each others blood
And drag each other's name through the dirt and the mud
Talk about and doubt your brother
Turn state evidence and sell out each other
Could it be fear, envy, jealousy or just confusion
Hopeless, ignorant, brothers misusing
Each other in ways that are misunderstood
Or could it be the fact that you are the rat from way back
And still up to no good
It shouldn't take another civil rights riot to have success
How many black leaders do we have to lay to rest
Before we clean up
Before we wake up and stop settling for less
(flick the switch, the power is on)
It's coming to you live
"it's not transmitting", "it's not televised"
We are not on the air, the power is out
If the enemy is not within my friend
Then what's all the peer pressure about
If we came together in perfect harmony
Then what would they have to say about us
Then what would their excuses be
If we came together in perfect harmony
Then how many of our young will be in the
     cemetery or the penitentiary
If we came together in perfect harmony
Just imagine the power, the peace and tranquility
If we can together in perfect harmony
What would life be like in our community, if
     we came together in harmony
(slick the switch, the power is on)
Behold how good and pleasant it is for brothers
To dwell together in unity

Continued

It's like the precious ointment upon the head
That ran down the beard, even Aaron's beard
That went down the skirts of his garment
As the dew that descended upon the mountains of Zion
For there the Lord commanded the blessings
Even life forever more
If we came together as one (the power is on, the power is on)
Oh happy days, oh happy days
When the saints go marching in
Most will be surprised
"My God", it's the revolution
If we came together – if we came together
In peace and unity
It's not a sign of power
There's power in numbers my brother
One early morning you're going to "wake up"
Wipe your eyes and turn on your TV
And then you are going to realize
There is power in unity
The revolution is finally being televised
And all the little white lies are being exposed
"we are on the air again"
"the power is one" "the power is on"
And everybody knows, and everybody knows
The peer pressure is gone
We flicked and switched up
And now the power is on
Things are not what they used to be
Change has come through unity
We've silenced the violence and help up on crime
It sounds good and it's coming all in good time
There's been an evaluation, a revolution
We've found another solution

Continued

Discrimination, segregation, it's not welcome in this nation
It's no longer an abomination for us to have an education
The states are united, "we are divided"
And everyone knows something is wrong
It's time to unite for what's right
(flick the switch, the power is on)
(the power is on) against police brutality,
     drug addiction and conspiracy
(the power is on) against the racist and the prejudice
(the power is on) for equal rights and opportunity
(the power is on) for fair trials in the court room
To shut down all the political deceivers
To stop the stereotype
And those who are out to mislead us, to stop us from doing right
Let's let the world know that these days of
     black on black crimes are gone
For we have flicked and switched up
Watch out world (the power's on) (the power's on)

I ONCE WAS BLIND
BUT NOW I SEE
THE FUTURE LOOKS GOOD FOR EVERY MAN

Looking at life through the eyes of a child
With faith and joy and a gentle smile
But as I grow older and become a man
The racism, the hate, I could never understand
Discrimination and segregation, society and racial tension
The white house war against the poor
Republicans, blacks and Christians
I once was blind but now I see
Private prisoners, house maids, and home slaves
Fire, brimstone and the horrors of hell
Descendents of slaves, the violence and silence
And things we were made never to tell
Walking in darkness seeking the light
Mississippi River lead me on
Beyond the sorrow, hate and death
Beyond the plantation where I was born
I can see the trails of blood from Washington, DC
The lynching and tension in Memphis, TN
The Birmingham scam
The raping and hating in slavery
The things we were robbed of
The things we were giving
The will power that kept us wanting to keep living

Continued

The tragic mistakes and violent outbreaks
We still stand with pride and loyalty of kings
In broken slave chains and poor people's campaigns
The demand is high to pioneer another coalition
To organize a committee particularly
For those who are blind and for those who will listen
I once was blind but now I see
The land of the rich, the land of the free
And the foolish scams you've played on me
Held down by political conspiracy
Ruler of darkness and powerful liars
With hidden tactics to create invisible chains
To hold us back and keep us struggling
Like pieces in a chess game
From Queen Elizabeth to King James
From the white house castle
To the smallest pawn
You will be conquered
And life will go on
So the revolution "will be" televised
When the world sees through your foolish lies
And all your social organizations of bigotry
Will come tumbling down
Like a Mississippi Valley
What the devil means for bad, God means for good
One day we will all understand
I once was blind, but now I see
The future looks good for every man.

GET HIGH?
DIE?
WHY?

One day we'll be in God's kingdom
Reminiscing about the past
All the good times we spent together
Just to get a laugh
I look forward to spending time with you
In our after life
Right now I'm gazing upon your tombstone
And I don't feel that nice
As my hopes for our heavenly gifts
Overcome my sorrow
It gives me the strength to continue on
And make it to tomorrow
On one hand I wish you all the best
After all that we've been through
On the other hand I'm sad you're gone
Because I'm missing you
I gaze into the sky searching for your spirit
I call your name in my prayers, hoping you can hear it
Remember how we used to talk about when we grow up
How we will do the same
You will name your son after me
And I'll give my son your name
Remember when you taught me how to play basketball
And to kept blocking my shot
I still believe I could have won that game
You can believe it or not
Why did you start getting high man?
Why did you separate us?
You left me all alone
Just for a quick rush

Continued

Now what am I going to do
I can't believe you're gone
In my heart you will always live
In me you will live on
You could have come and talked with me
If you were having problems
Getting high just gave you more
What? You thought that getting high would solve them?
I still have the last picture we took
Sitting on my dresser at home
But now the only thing I can picture
Is your name on the tombstone
Why did you start getting high man?
You didn't need that stuff
All the love you had in your life
Wasn't that enough
Now your poor children
Growing up without a dad
Most of the people at your funeral just shook their heads
And said "Man, that's too bad".
Your mother outlived you
How do you think she feels?
When you got high, did you think it was OK?
"Boy, be for real"
One day we will be together again
In that great mansion beyond the sky
Then maybe you can explain to me, "Why?" "Big Brother"
"Why did you start getting high?"

D. Washington

POP THE HUSTLER

Never put your children
In the street game of death and destruction
They will end up just like you did
An egotistical kid, stubborn with nothing
Young and in prison, self-centered, addicted to drugs and very
Argumentative and manipulative
What you taught him only got him aggression
Miserable and destructive, anger and violence
And when someone mentions love, he stands in silence
He's good at playing mind games with selfish ambitions
Living day for day, most days he so broke
He can't even pay attention
When you taught him how to hang and demand his respect
You taught him how to hang with a noose on his neck
Street games and prison chains give you nothing but pain
A reckless life is a sacrifice, six feet under, back from where you came
Pop the Hustler, Pop the Hustler
Someone with a gun is bound to Pop the Hustler
Troubled families, abusive, addicted, broken homes
Will push a child to learn from the street
There he will be deceived and mislead then left alone
Until life says, now I lay me down to sleep
The consequences are unpredictable and inappropriate
Life is hard, the streets are rough, and no one is considerate
He only wanted to be like Pop the Hustler with the girls
The clothes, the cars
But he never saw behind the door, the suffering, the prison bars
Never put your children in the street game
Of death and destruction
Cause he will end up just like you did
Burned out, played out, old with nothing
Fast hustling money will always get the best of you
The night life is not the right life for the smart
It's the life for the lost
It ain't no fun when the victim got the gun

In the court room, on the stand
When the DA asks the witness is he here
And the victim says "yes, that's the man"
When all you've hustled for is instantly taken away in one day
And Pop the Hustler got warrants so he can't come to court
To watch them take you away
So don't teach your children
The street games of death and destruction
Cause someone is bound to Pop the Hustler
And leave everyone with nothing
They say I'm accountable for my own actions Daddy
They say that I should accept the blame
Yet I was young without direction
Then you taught me the game
I made a lot of money
I've harmed the innocent
I've left some women poor and homeless
Even pregnant
There's been times when I was thankful
And times when I felt sorrow
Today I plan to hustle, but what's my plans for tomorrow
Should I teach my children
The things I learned from you
Would they grow up, blind by the glamour
And one day, someone with a gun, is bound to
Pop the Hustler, Pop the Hustler
Never teach your children the street game
Of death and destruction
Cause if they're lucky
They will end up
Word?? down
With nothing
And if they continue to live
In the lifestyle you taught them
Someone is bound
To Pop the Hustler
Pop the Hustler.

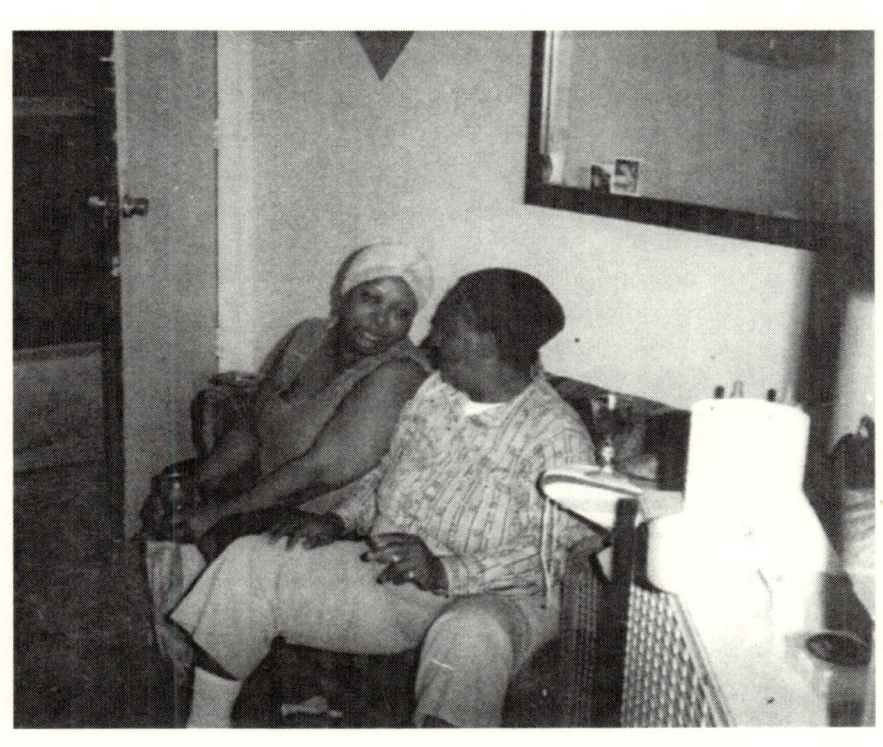

MA-MA I TRIED TO STAY STRONG
BUT I JUST BROKE DOWN AND CRIED

Ma-Ma, Ma-Ma
Always by my side, and there when I need you
Whether right or wrong, beside me you stood strong
No matter what I have to go through
You've bore the pain from my birth
And all the other stuff I put you through in life
Just so I can have happy holidays
You pressed down and even sacrificed
Living in low income housing, hand-me-down clothes and welfare
You've done the best and struggled
Even when you combed my nappy hair
I cried and screamed but I knew you cared
From that look in your eyes and the good times we shared
From fish and grits, to black eyed peas and collard greens
You taught me well, how to cook and how to look
In my big brothers jeans
Gave me stability, opened my eyes to reality
Showed me responsibility, surrounded by negativity
You gave me the key so I can have the capability
To be who I could be
In this world that wants to keep me, pressed down in poverty
So I cried
When I went to court for trial
You gave me that gentle smile

Continued

And that hug of love, when I was dope sick and half dead
You put a roof over my head
And I will never forget the tears that you shed
On that day when they took me away
Ma-Ma, Ma-Ma
So I cried
I cried because first you were happy that I was caught
Because I should have been dead and I had enough
I cried because if you died then I will have
    to stand over you in handcuffs
I cried because I know you have done your best and I failed
I cried because I knew I wasn't the only one going to jail
I cried because I knew I was the one you used to depend on
I cried because I knew one day I'll turn around
    and realize Ma-Ma is gone
It had nothing to do with home girl
Because I knew she would not last
It had nothing to do with being afraid because
Well, you know my past
It had nothing to do with the judge, the jury or the DA
It had nothing to do with the lawyer or what the witness had to say
It had nothing to do with my lifestyle
Because I "knew" I had enough
I pictured myself standing over your casket
Shackled up and handcuffed
"SO, I CRIED"
Always by my side and there when I needed you
Whether right or wrong, beside me you stood strong
No matter what I had to go through
Lord God in heaven above

Continued

Don't take my Ma-Ma away
She's been my only true friend
And this is what I pray
I cried because you tried to help and there was nothing you could do
I cried because you had to know how much I truly love you
Tears slowly filled my eyes
And rolled down my face
That hollow, empty feeling I felt
Can never be replaced
I look into your eyes Ma-ma
With shame, guilt and sorrow
You looked back with love and said
"I'll be up to see you tomorrow"
You've always given me hope
And so quick to forgive
You've been the strength I've always needed
To stand and want to live
And at my trial I wanted to stay strong
"I really truly tried"
But when I thought of all I put you through
Ma-ma
I just broke down and cried
I just broke down and cried.

GOD REUNITE ME AND MY SON

Dear Son
How can I explain to you why I could not be there?
I know you've had your hopes and dreams
Your cries and your prayers
I could start by expressing
How life is so unfair
The prisons, the drugs, the crimes, the racism
And people who just don't care
How I tried to hold onto you from behind these
Prison walls
With bitter stressful feelings, relationships and
Collect phone calls
How I reached out to your Mother
As she moved on in silence
How I cried to the parole board
But my record had too my violence
The plans I had for you and I since you were a little kid
But Daddy made mistakes
And Daddy caught a bid
I know you've heard a lot of things and you've
Tried to understand
Maybe you won't until you experience life's struggles
When you become a man
I've played the hand life dealt to me

Continued

I did my best with the hand I had
I will always love you son
Sincerely, Your Dad
There's a bond between a father and his son
That could never be broken
Like Abraham and Isaac
A bond since the word of God was spoken
So no matter what happens in life
Whether they love us
Whether they hate us
You are a special part of me
And no one can separate us
I wanted to be there with you
On Christmas and your birthday
But I have to wait for my release date
And for God to make a way
I wished to be with you
And do the things you like
To teach you how to skateboard
Play ball and ride a bike
I've made bad choices son
And with that I had to pay
And God willing, I'll have the chance
To make it up one day
I pray you don't hate me
For the wrong that I've done
Try to stay strong
It won't be long
For God to reunite me and my son.

MANUFACTURED AND PRODUCED
AS AN AMERICAN

Slayed and betrayed by society
Look into my mind, tell me what you see
Bricks and bars of another penitentiary
Hate a man, enslave a man
And I can't fight it
Looking in the mirror and am undecided
Trying to figure out who the hell I am
Manufactured and produced as an American

The thoughts that I think are of the Bible
The world wants to label me unreliable
I've always got to go the extra mile
Institutionalized for a little while
The agreement that I got is indestructible
You don't fuck with me and I won't fuck with you
I mood swing, like a suicidal dope feen
I ruff-ruff like a boogie man on Halloween
You think you know me but you still can't understand
Because I'm not your average everyday American

Some may even label me to be a refugee
Some may call me a nigger or a want to be
But until you sat down and read my diary
All you know about me is what you see "g"
I'm not a black man, I'm not an African
Who am I, what am I?
Manufactured and produced as an American
My eyes are on fire, my muscles are tight
My heart is numb
Who am I, Where am I, Where did I come from?

A COTTON PICKING SHAME

Through blood, sweat and tears
Oppressed for four hundred and thirty five years
We all need somebody to lean on
Fertilize the tree and keep the roots strong
Pikaninnie working the cotton field
Overseer said "I'll make you a good deal"
"If you work as hard as you work the field, in my house
The same food I eat will be in your mouth"
Little Hymie left his friends and family
And moved into a world of vanity
To end up in a state of insanity
They made him work real hard for the master
It was like a good life sentence, on and after
Clean linens, clean clothes and a fresh bath
Sometimes he gets so happy he just laughs
Not thinking about those he left behind
Picking cotton night and day eating nothing but swine
He even said he was better than the cotton picker
Because they call him by name and not little nigger
So he wondered what happened to the house
    nigger that worked before me
He must have worked so good that the master set him free
If I please my master maybe
I'll get my freedom card
The next time my master let me beat a slave
I'll whip him extra hard
So he whipped some and hung some from a tree
He said he will do anything for the dream of being free

Continued

The young brother didn't think about the law of gravity
What goes up must come down
Or the three hundred and sixty degrees
What goes around comes around
Now years gone past, the house nigger is now an old man
The master said "I give him an order and he
        looks like he don't understand"
He's just old and worthless like a fruit gone rotten
So the master ordered the house nigger back to picking cotton
Back on the fields where he started from
He looked for his friends but he had none
When he died he left as an old lonely man
Someone who forgot he was and African
All he wanted was to succeed, he didn't mean no harm
Institutionalized by an oppressed system he became an Uncle Tom
The moral to this story is plain
It's OK to climb the ladder but don't forget from where you came
And never burn the bridges that you cross
Cause you might try to go back and get lost
Do unto others as you would have them do unto you
And try to help those who are still picking cotton too
Cause you never miss your water until your wells dry
And you don't want to be old and lonely before you die.

PASSION

Hey young man – what's on your mind
So you think its cool to be the show off kind
Always loud and putting other people down
Drinking and acting like a clown
Respect is what you want from the hood
And you seek to be satisfied anyway you could
People smile in your face and you think they really love you
But you would rather believe a lie than to face what is true
Just soothe yourself by smoking weed, drinking beers
Doing your dirt and driving your cars
Being more than willing to hide behind anything
Than face what you really are
Afraid to fight anything or anybody up and up and one on one
If you can't hide behind your boys, you run and get a gun
Call yourself a real trooper on the block
Always want to prove you got the biggest penis and the most heart
You even disrespect your elders cause you think you're a man
Because you got a girl pregnant, she had a little boy
And he calls you Dad
Your girls on welfare, you're living with her mama
You drop out of school, got no job
And still you think you're bad

Continued

With your chest puffed up, showing your chain
Like you're down with the big boys and ahead of the game
Yah – you done it all, seen it all, there's nothing you can't do
People dying on the streets but that will never happen to you
So you can get drunk, drive your car and still make it home
Shoot dope, smoking cocaine, party all night, you're never alone
So I came to visit you at the hospital with this black rose
To put in your hands
Someone told me you had HIV
I didn't believe them but now I understand
After running people's lives and breaking up home after home
I stand and look down on you, dying all alone
So where's your home boys, you know, the ones that partied,
Smiled, had fun and laughed
I guess they just rolled over, so you can kiss their ass
Oh, but you didn't lose everything
Knowledge is what you gained
What comes around, goes around
And one night of passion
Can give you a life of pain.

Photo Section

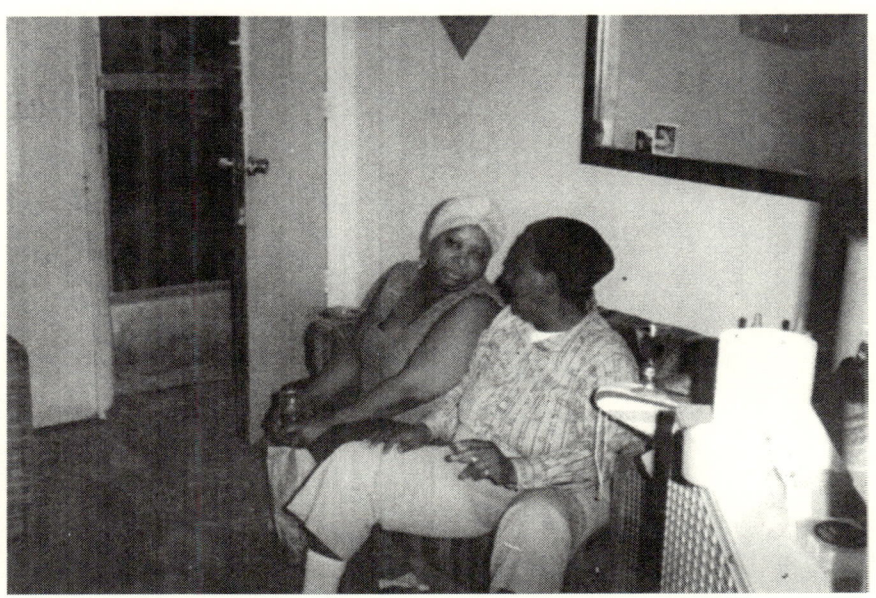

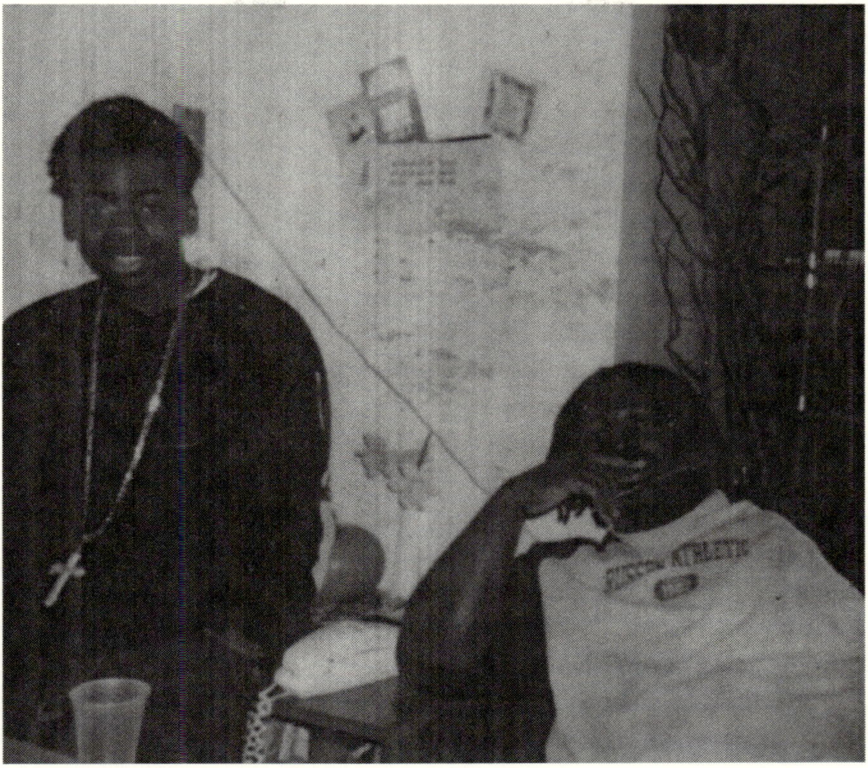

NO BLAME – NO SHAME

I was raised in a project on welfare
My mother was the only one that did care
I used to steal bikes just to have one
I used to jack other kids just for fun
I never had anyone to look up to
But the players on the corner and the drug crew
I used to go to gas stations for a job
But my address in the project made it hard
I saw Super Fly at the movies
He had a style of his own, that moved me
So I turned into a stick-up kid
And I tried to have everything that Super Fly did
I've been in and out of jail all my life
The game I was playing had set dice
It's just a check mate, no win situation
I even started taking medication
Cause the white man told me I ain't right
And according to his world, I'm a parasite
So I want to seek help from the black man
If no one can't, my own will understand
A brother tried to kill me cause I was on his block
I guess he thought I tried to stick him for a white rock
If everybody is blind, who can see
Man, this peer pressure is killing me
Even among my own there's segregation
That's what the white man wants, separation

Continued

Like a puzzle of the world with an extra piece
Round and round it goes, just never cease
In and out, up and down, and around again
Looking for a space on this puzzle for a young black man
Where else in this world would I fit
Besides jail or the war zone project
So I became somebody when I joined a gang
We had our own block and respect for our name
I had money every day, made it day and night
I had more than the white man and I'm a parasite
They just got more troops, but it's all the same
Sometimes I reminisce on the past
I think about stealing bikes and I laugh
My cousins that were raised in the suburbs
They wouldn't touch a drink nor smoke herb
One even got a job as a policeman
Is there a piece in this puzzle for an African
My cousin is a cop and I don't doubt
That he will cuff me up too cause he's a sell out
My life was always hard and full of shit
Now I'm just the black man from the projects
Now I sit in a jail cell and try to fight
A system that considers me a parasite
The doctors want to give me medication
Another check mate in a no win situation
So I try to make changes that are right
Like go to church on Sunday and Wednesday nights
But the picture shows Jesus as white
How can a black brother get tight

Continued

With a white picture that never did care
For a black man from the project on welfare
So I pray to Jesus who is not white nor black
And I patiently wait for him to come back
And forgive me for believing the lie
That I can live and die like Super Fly
The world is not a puzzle, it's a painting
It's not the white man, it's Satan
It don't matter where you're from, it's where you're at
Don't do what I did, just learn from that
Now the morale to my story is clear
You can make it out of the project, off welfare
But if you take the wrong road like I did
There's a casket or a jail cell waiting for you kid
Don't be hard headed, take my advice
Don't blame another man for what you did in life
Believe in God and never forget to pray
Life is what you make of it and crime doesn't pay
It doesn't matter where you are from but where you are at
And you can be someone others can look up to, believe that
And don't get caught up in all that racist, systematic
Shift the blame shit
If they make it from the suburbs
YOU can make if from the projects.

NO BLAME
NO SHAME

114

I CAN SUCCEED

I can be successful
I can overcome
One day at a time
Victory shall be mine
To stand and say I won

I owe it to myself, for the joy I have enhanced
To treat myself good
Like I've always should
And to give myself a chance

And if I ever fall
Or make a small mistake
I dust myself off the best way I can
I'll do whatever it takes

Cause I can be successful
As any; other man
I don't have to settle
For the lower level
Over and over again
I can learn to love myself
And to treat myself with respect
And not run away
Or wake up the next day
In jail with shame and regret

I can be successful
Clean and serene
I don't have to be high to succeed
I'll humble myself
And ask someone else
To give me to the tools that I need

Continued

No more dirty floors
Or sleeping outdoors
Or ripping and running for days
No more selling myself short
With no support
And taking chances with AIDS

Cause I can be successful
I believe in change
I can face life's problems and fears
I don't have to stuff my feelings and get high
I can face them and cry
Blow my nose and wipe away my tears

I'd rather wipe my face
Then to live in a place
Like prison or six feet under
Like a man should
Than to be institutional and wonder

If I could change
Can I over come
Would victory be mine
Would I have ever one
Could I point and blame someone else
What would be the blame
Booze and cocaine
For the things that I've done to myself

The choice is mine
And that's guaranteed
The ball is in my hand
To fail or succeed
Or even give it a try

Continued

Yet I can succeed
It's also guaranteed
If I don't try
The changes are great
I would die

I have a right to be happy
A need to be content
A want to stop inflicting
Self-punishment

Compassion
And aggression, mixed emotions
Is it me
The consequences are too hard to bear
I looked yet could not find
The one's I left behind
And those who are here don't care

So with angry energy
I fight to be free
From this wicked addicted behavior

For the drugs that penetrated my mind
And motivated my life in time
Became my Lord and my savior

I can murder and hide
Or commit suicide
My life is one big problem

Or I can learn the rules
Pick up the tools
Work on my problems and solve them

Why settle for less
When I can do my best
For what is guaranteed
After my whole life
Was a senseless sacrifice
"Finally I can succeed"

HEAVENLY ARTIST

All mighty power, creator
Of all living things
The sun shines, the plants grow, the birds sing
In darkness the stars sparkle
The moon glows great light

The mountains, the waters, divided just right

The raindrops, the snowflakes, the rainbow
The whispering in the wind
The soul, the spirit and the heavens

Created by my creator
Of the earth and heavens above
God of peace, God of mercy, God of power, God of love

In the garden, my God created man
He molded me with sand and held him in his mighty hand
With the breath of life and all the love one can give

God created man in his image
A living soul, wonderfully made
By the most creative God
We live....

We were made by Him, through Him and for Him
And without Him we cannot exist
Spoken into existence by the word of God
And gifted with life, molded in love, mighty creator
My heavenly artist.

FAITHFUL FOR SURE
GOD WON'T JUDGE YOU!

Don't you judge me, for the wrong you may think I do
For God is the judge and believe me, he won't misjudge you
We are not your enemy and we're not God,
    consider the source of course
We got enough enemies in me to make my
    own life hard, so stop trying
To knock down the church by suing me as a pawn
Cause whether you come or not, the work of the Lord will still go on
It makes no difference whether I drink milk or you eat meat
Cause we're in the same back alleyway trying to make it to his
Golden streets.
God saved your soul, just like he saved me, so stop exulting yourself
You're not the only one he set free, and if you ever got the chance
To see me fall, don't gossip about it, pray for me, "that's all"
I showed you love and you rejected it
I tried to be peaceful and you couldn't accept it
Let me ask you a question
What would you do and what would you say,
    if Jesus should walk in here today?
Would you love me?
Would you hug me?
Could we bow our heads and pray?
Or would you treat him like you treat me in your ungodly way?
How could you love me and misjudge me then
    hold my hand and call me "brother"
Smile at me, like we were at peace with each other
If Jesus should walk in this place today, tell me, what would you do?

Continued

What would you say?
Would you say, Lord, the man next to me is a snitch or a skinner?
But "me" I'm OK
"I'm only a sinner"
Would you treat him like you treat me, in your ungodly way?
Tell me, what would you do, what would you say?
I've been persecuted, talked about, knocked
    down, but not knocked out
So what have you got to say?
Can't keep me down, I know life is not fair
What I got to say will first be said, in prayer, so don't judge me
For the wrong you may think I do, for God is
    the judge and believe me, he won't
Misjudge you, faithful for sure, God won't misjudge you.
We all fall short of the glory of God, sometimes we fall easy
Sometimes we fall hard
I will never take you through temptations you cannot bear
Says the Lord of the host, who already has been there
Love thy neighbor just as you loved me,
    without love you have nothing
So how can you be free
Repent from your sins, for the kingdom of God is at hand
For it my people that are called by my name
    come, then I will heal their land
Blessed is the man who is persecuted for righteousness sake
So call me hypocrite, call me fake, you can mix sinners with saints
And still have death
You can mix war with hate, and end up with a mess
You can mix sand with stone and call it a grave
But when you mix Christians with the love of God
You'll be amazed
So let's stop judging one another and putting each other down
For we stand in the site of God on holy ground
Let God be the judge
His judgment is fair and true
No matter what you say, no matter what you do
FAITHFUL FOR SURE, *"GOD WON'T MISJUDGE YOU!!!"*

LIKE A CHILD OF GOD

As I sit in the dirt
I lean back on a tree
And wonder how many slaves hung here seeking to be free
I gaze upon the children, how they run, laugh and play
Not knowing the joys of being a child will slowly fade away
I think about the courtrooms, mankind and his greed
Where life is not a special thing nor is it guaranteed
I think about the system and how evil one can be
They give and take, the phony handshakes, and the threat of reality
I thought about the politicians and how they plan the game
From one political lie, a whole nation could
    die, and yet they have no shame
Then a bird flew over my head and I wondered, was he free
Some have houses, some have cages, just like you and me
I could not find anything around that I can see that is free
The law of man, the law of nature, even gravity
Then I looked into the heavens and I said to myself "gee"
After all this time of working my mind, it was right in front of me
I'll just ask God, he sets captives free
The Bible says if I ask he will deliver me

Continued

So I prayed and asked the Lord, as I looked into the sky
A voice came down from heaven
It said, my son, do what I've done
Just take your cross and die
There is therefore no condemnation to those who walk in Christ
I don't mean suicide, I mean spiritual for life
The law of sin and death
No longer have a hold on me
For the law of the spirit of life in Christ
Has set the captive free
As I sit in this dirt
I lean back on a tree
And wonder how many slaves just hung here
Seeking to be free
How many were set free, how many will realize
Just ask God
It's not hard for him to open your eyes
How many did accept him
How many did reject him
How many are still lost, how many just sat
    here, how many walked away
And those that found freedom in Christ, will run, laugh and play.

THE LAW OF GOD
AGAINST THE LAW OF MAN

The time is coming when loving Jesus
Would be against mans law
The prisons would be full of Christians
And the street full of violent men
Some churches would still be preaching
Falsehood is what they would be teaching
People would be ignorant; no one would be in fear
Lost and on their way to hell and neither would they care
Halloween holidays and praise Santa Clause
The Easter Bunny and the Christ on there cross
No sin and salvation preached, and no one
    dare preach Christ has risen
Colored corn and big birds, would be the symbol
For thanks given
Christians with the anointing of the Holy Spirit
Would be called mentally insane
There'll even be a price to pay for using Jesus' name
Worshipping saints and statues of Gods that are not even real
Would you give into the laws of man
Or would you go to jail
Are you like Peter, Paul or John
Or are you like Judas Iscariot
If your Bible was illegal
Would you break the law or carry it

The time is coming when shame
Would be a big game
The devil would use to keep us from walking with Christ
Those of us not rooted in his word
Wouldn't even sacrifice
Friends on the street wouldn't understand
So you don't tell them that you're a Christian.

PICKED UP AND LET DOWN

Peer pressure, undermined, degraded, enslaved by law
The white pony, the pink elephants
Orange sunshine, black beauties, the bald headed eagle, the claw
In a world of bigotry, ignorance, poverty, greed, lust and death
Just too much weight for one man
So you try to debate and find no escape
In a world that is educated by a system you just can't understand
If you had your own little corner
Where you can live like you want to
And not be examined by others
In a scientific way, to see how you exist
So your heart grows hard
And your head just nods
Cause you just can't adapt in a world like this
So where can you go when you're brought so low
In a world of hatred and people of fear
You failed but tried to fit in, you even lied
And deep in your soul, you know, you're not welcome here

Continued

You need to be accepted by someone
Either stand for something or fall
So you started doing drugs and got hooked
And you finally escaped after all
Peer pressure, undermined, degraded, enslaved
By a mind altering, mood changing substance
That once you set free
Now deceived and tricked off, fond and lost
You find that things that set you free
Can also put you in captivity
And it was better just to run with reality
In a fast world that you could never fit in
Than to be chasing drugs in a never ending war
Fighting a battle that you can never win
All your life you dreamed to be free
And you finally made it, the road was rough
And times were always hard
For the last time society lets you down
As your casket disappears in the graveyard
He's been chasing drugs most of his life
Looking for a paradise
But one hell of a guy when he was high.

MURDER, MAYHEM AND MYSTERY

Am I the criminal or the victim in this white collar war?
We are constantly fighting, got the ghetto in an uproar
And the minority men are not uniting.
How can it rain constantly and why does it
    always end up a dreary day?
For the first time in the height of my life, it snowed
    all night long in the month of May.
The highway traffic was so thick we couldn't even see the white lines
So I pulled over to a rocky road just to unload until things died down
As I knew they would
It's not just a coincidence that the substance is
    always recognized in the ghetto hood
Just another long night and a hard, long, lonely road to travel
For a loving man like me
Always looking for the freedom in my country, tis
    the sweet land of liberty I never see
As the globe goes around and some seem to always go uphill
Could it be this highway or is it just another way to get high?
Constantly picking up speed as I am coming down
Lost on a dead-end street in a strange land and a foreign town
Every street light is green, just what does this mean?
I've never experienced anything in life like this before
My brakes just stopped working!
By body is shaking, going berserk, and I want more, I want more!
The snow was coming down and the road was very icy
I started to swerve and I knew that this might be a swerve too strong
Or a curve too long

Continued

Then crack, bam, boom, smack, then a crack
    raid crash, my legs had no feeling
And the neck on nip was melting like it had whiplash!
The highway got worse and the snow came down bad
I thought that one more exhale was all that I had
I blacked out and it was so strange how I changed
Like Jekyll and Hyde on my inside
I felt like I murdered a good man, the only man in my cell block,
In an empty jail
And on my last exhale I knew that I'd never walk again
How did I get lost on this highway? The signs were so large,
The reflection was so strong, how did I not see?
The Murder, Mayhem and my life is such a Mystery to me
Looking for the right exit I was taken for another ride
I got lost jut hoping one day soon I'll make
    it back from a long hard crash
And I still try to cope with the after effects from the crack
Am I a criminal or the victim? Can I blame
    society for the majority of the
Minority caught up in war?
That's such an uproar of Murder, Mayhem and Mystery
The blind road was so cold, I just couldn't
    see through the rain, the snow,
The sleet and the hail
From bondage in the flesh to freedom in
    the grave, and if I'm lucky I'll
Just end up shackled in chains and locked up in jail
With all the ifs, ands and buts and excuses in
    my mind about being confined
I shouldn't have to do time

Continued

Excuses like
Someone else was driving my car, I picked up a hitch-hiker and I was
Mentally, emotionally and physically attacked!
Didn't you see me jumping lanes? Blowing my horn and yelling
"Car Jack – Car Jack"
I don't care how bad the traffic is I'm never going
    to pull over to a rocky road again
Or will I fight in a war with snowballs and
    rocks, in a battle already lost
Thinking I can win?
I've had it all, I've done it all and now I have nothing!
If I had two peas in a pod, at least I'll have a little something
Living in this prison, what can a man do?
Now what he wants to do!
Now when he wants to!
Man, I don't even have me
In the next move to be made in this game of
    monopoly is such a mystery!
I roll the dice in my life, it's a gamble, I try to
    pass go yet always end up in jail
So don't take bad chances
Don't drive in a blizzard, black ice or hail
Don't let the blind lead you
Don't pick up hitch-hikers
And don't live a lie.
You see, there are no winners in this war
We all do, we all die
I can't blame the next man and the next man can't blame me
First Murder, now Mayhem, it's such a mystery
Am I the criminal or the victim? And who is a menace to society?
There is a story that is true and there is a story
    untold, like a man like me
Traveling down this same blind road....of MURDER,
    MAYHEM AND MYSTERY.

Written and Produced by
Daniel J. Washington

129

KICKED OUT AND TRAPPED
A VICIOUS CYCLE

Kicked out of the crack house and back in the street
I got no money, my body is hungry
And I ain't took a bath in about a week
My eyes are wide open and I'm on alert
On guard for my enemies cause I do dirt
Something in my head said, go to the shelter and stay
But I'm chasing my high and I got to get paid
Now I'm back on the drive through block
Where you can just drive up, roll your window down and cop um
Just standing on the corner full of hope
That the dealers don't catch me out here selling soap
If a dealer don't catch me, a customer will
So I scratched my dirty ass and said, "man, I got to chill"
I've been in and out of jail all my life
I even contemplated suicide and rolled the death dice
Smoking don't make me a bad guy
I got it all under control and I can handle my high
My mother don't want me at her house
She told everyone I stole her VCR, man, she's got a big mouth
I'll go back to the shelter but it's too late
I'll go back to get some food but they already ate
What the hell am I going to do tonight
I'm tired of picking particles off the floor and to try and
Smoke it on my pipe
So business is bad and the night is slow
I'm kicked out of the crack house with no place to go
I looked across the street at the corner store
If I can rob that place I won't be hungry no more

Continued

130

I robbed the store, I didn't take no food to eat
I just wanted to get high and keep running the street
With a pocketful of money I'm back at the crack house
Everyone's sitting around the table quiet as a church mouse
When I was broke they kicked me out, now they want me to stay
Someone will probably try to kill me if I try to walk away
So I just sat at the table and smoked
Rock after rock until I became broke
Kicked out of the crack house once again
Sweating, dirty and my body's stinking
The sun came up and it beamed bright
I'm weak because I've been up getting high all night
The shelter won't let me have a bed until five
And if I had one more hit, man, I can come alive
So I went back to the corner and I found
A car drive up with its window down
So I sold him some soap and sent him on his way
Now I'm back at the crack house welcome to stay
I had a couple of drinks and sex with a whore
Smoked up all my money and then they
        made me go back out the door
Just when I walked out of the house someone shot me
I thought I was too slick but they got me
Hit me in the back with a forty-five
The last words I heard was, "Is he alive – Is he alive".
I woke up in the hospital, happy to be alive
Until the doctor came in and told me I've been paralyzed
I said to myself, "it just ain't fair"
First I'm kicked out of the crack house
Now I'm trapped in a wheel chair. A VICIOUS CYCLE.

D. Washington

RELAPSE

Hey Mr. Puppeteer, I've been locked up far too long
Do your thing, pull my strings
While I dance to the beat of another sad song
Take me higher above this crowd so I can see
Give me your grace beyond this place
Let's go to another galaxy
Federal taxes and capital rates, the extraordinary
　　pressures of everyday life
Help me escape this love and hate
Let's go lay in paradise
I'm a chemist just for today
Taking research while I play
Mr. Puppeteer, take me down
Now I'm tired, give me some rest
My eyes look wired, my throat is dry
And my heart is banging out of my chest
I ran out of money, pull my strings
Lead me on to get some more
I need a gun, let's go get one
So we can rob the liquor store
Big butt woman can I trick
Let's go somewhere we can lay
When my hopes and dreams are gone
Promise me that you would stay
Back in my box locked up again
Crying out conspiracy
It's not my fault Mr. Puppeteer man
Pull my strings and set me free
All up in one puff of smoke
One more young wasted life
Looking after my puppet master
Causes me to sacrifice
Can I exist with no strings attached
Play that beat so I can dance
Take me up so I can relax
And give me just one more chance
Let me dance to just one more song
Cause I've been locked up far too long.

FEEL ME

Whores gone wild
Streets gone mad
Young brothers calling each other nigger
Today they call it slang

Here's a gun
Never shot one
Baby dies
Mother cries
Another stray bullet
Must have been a street gang

Water breaks on the main line
Crack pipe
Rocks coming down
Chasing and running
Looking for my first love
Here I am
Buy jumpsuits in jail
What's the deal
Feel me

Dead men tell no tales
To tears in a bucket
Mother fuck it
Can't get no vain
To understand the living
You've got to commune with the dead
So I stay high
You feel me

Continued

This is a cash and carry world
So I pay as I go
Sometimes I pay a little
Sometimes I pay a lot
You got a light
Mr. Dope Man
Let me have just one more shot
I'll come back down
You got my word
Feel me

Left behind, lost in time
Cold steel, bricks and concrete
I'm back, call on the mainline
Just one last time
Yes, like such
A little too much
Good bye, farewell
Cruel world
Come back, come back
Good shit, good bye
One deal you do, you die
Listen to the mother cry
One hell of a guy
Lived a lit
Farewell, good bye
You feel me.

FAST CHANGE GOT THE BEST OF ME

Fresh out of the joint with a brand new start
Back on the block, trying to make the best with what little I got
Filling out job applications but they're all denied
I have no history or experiences except for what I've done inside
I can pick up cigarette butts, stand up for count and watch TV
Well I did go to school, I got my GED
But these applications are asking for high school diplomas
Or a college degree
I can cook from a hot pot
And make a good cup of Kool Aid
I can also go back to my old block, pump dope and get paid
But I left jail telling myself I'm going to succeed
Yah, life is what you make it but nothing is guaranteed
Thank God I saved up enough money in jail to get my own crib
But next month when I can't pay rent, then where will I live?
I can find me a girl that's on welfare and move into her place
But I want a brand new start, not another
     rate race in someone else's space
My back's against the ropes and I'm losing the fight
Between a rock and a hard place and I only want to do what's right
A man's got to do what he must to survive
I should have just faced reality instead I fantasized
Thinking I can make it in a world of constant stereotype
Where I can't trust no man, whether black or white
All I need is a job to earn an honest pay
But they just look at me, shake their head and slowly walk away

Continued

The same man that did my drugs and tricked off with my whores
Won't trust me enough to give me a job, clean
     windows or open his doors
So I did all I could cause I've been all I can be
I'm back on the block, punching my clock
Dealing dope, will I get caught, I hope I don't
Cause fast change ain't no robbery
It is cool to slip burgers and shake fries
And believe the lies
Or is it cool to pay my rent, dress slick
Drive my cars, BMWs and Jaguars
I do what I have to, to survive
Fast change ain't no robbery
But it will always get the best of me without a clue
I'm back in the courtrooms but I did what I had to do
Am I a victim of circumstance
Or a man who never had a chance
So I sit here in the courthouse gazing at 12 people ready to judge me
Most likely I'll be found guilty
Then the judge will determine whether to lock me up or set me free
Yet, no one was there when I couldn't find a job
No one was there when I was praying to God
To bless me with money so I can eat
And to give me the strength to make it to the street
No one was there when I sung the blues
Walking in the snow with holes in my shoes

Continued

No one was there when I shed my tears
I've been hated and rejected, for years and years
No one was there when I cried out for help
Fast change ain't no robbery, but what is its result?
Am I a victim of circumstance, a reject of society?
Fast change ain't no robbery, but it always got the best of me
I'm sitting in my jail cell facing a lot of time
Lonely, confused and mad
With vengeance on my mind
Teardrop don't come down because my heart is to hard to cry
My willpower is too strong to hang myself and die
So who commits the crimes and who is really free
Is your politics and traditions reality or robbery
Does this system that you set up help the rich and the poor
Or does the rich keep getting richer and the poor die in war?
You're a thief and I'm a thief, let's face reality
You rob, steal and kill politically
And the fast change I make to savor, it ain't no robbery
I'm not guilty, not as society
Fast change ain't no robbery
Yet it always got the best of me, it always got the best of me.

Trust and betrayal
Passion or conspiracy
Reality and robbery
Need or greed
Everyone will like to succeed
Yah, life is what you make it
But nothing is guaranteed – but robbery
It always got the best of me
Looking for a fast change in society

D. Washington

BASE

Now this little story must be heard
By the next generation so pass the word
About a young juvenile who tried to be a man
He quit school for hustlin'
He was a peddler, a pusher, a pocketbook taker
A player with the ladies and a cold heart breaker
Until one night when he faced inflation
He ran out of money while cocaine basin'
He was beginning all the bases for a piece of the rock
You see once you hit the pipe it's hard to stop
He fell to his knees like a man unstable
Hunting for a hit from the floor to the table
Then he ran out of the house, really feeling down
With no money in his pockets and his chin to the ground
Then he went home and got his heat
Ran across the block, down a dead end street
Kicked in the door to the liquor store and said
"This is a stick up, everybody on the floor"
Five minutes later he was out of the place
With two grand in his hand and his head on base
So he ran into the bathroom all alone
Chewing that pipe like a dog with a steak bone
Hit after hit, he couldn't stop, 24/7, around the clock
The first thing in the morning the cops kicked in the door
And there he was just lying on the floor
With a glass pipe in his hand
And cocaine on his nose
His eyes were open but his heart was froze
And that is the end of my story about cocaine basin'
Take it and pass it on to the next generation.

D. Washington

TO A CHILD WHO LIVES ALONE

Have you ever been so lonely that you felt that know one cared?
Did you ever feel like crying, but new you'd get know were
Have you ever wondered God why me' why me'
Have you ever tried to imaginate; even
    hallucinate, just to escape reality
Know body hears your cry, know body knows your pain
Have you ever lived with a bunch of strangers,
    who bailey know your name
Have you ever had to pray, God give me a home
I have know mommy or know daddy and I am alone
Have you ever contemplated suicide just to get some one to listen?
Have you ever acted out in anger just to get attention?
Have you ever had to wonder, what does mom look like
I wish I had a dad to teach me how to ride a bike
If you have never felt these things, God has smiled your way
Because there are children who feel these pains every single day
Have you ever thought about sharing some of your wealth?
Have you ever thought that God has blessed you,
    so you can be a blessing to someone elts
Have you ever thought about adopting to make your house a home?
To give a hug and show some love
to a child who lives alone

An apology from all fathers to all sons who have
    been victimized by this unfair world
And confused by this life.
Actions and consequences have made major changes
    in our lives and we act out in anger
With the unanswered question 'why'

Dear son i 'apologize'

Most black homes are dysfunctional
Not just because of drug use and abuse
But also for the simple fact that dad is not there and mom is
    trying her best to fill both shoes of being mom and dad.
The question is 'why'?
Why is dad not there'?

I remember going to the bank as a tanager and
    opening my first checking account
I didn't know anything about managing money
And growing up we did not have much
But when i figured out that i can go to the store and get stuff without
    having eny money in my account to cover my check i took
    advantage of it and that's when i first messed my credit up.
In this world your success in having much is limited with bad credit
So my son that's one of the reasons why you
    did not have the house to live in
Or maybe a new car when you got your license, or all
    of the other stuff you saw the middle or high class
    get there children, and because of that act
I apologize.

I remember going to this gas station for my very
    first job when i became of age to work
The boss i believe he really took a liken to me, I mean we
    talked for a while and then he pulled out my application,
    when he saw that my address was one from the projects
    across the street he did not give me the job.

So after some time went by I just got frustrated, gave up and started
    a life of crime, I mean it seemed as if all of the criminals around
    me adapted to that life and some seem to be doing well.
I didn't look behind the black Curtin,
The court dates, the cheating and unfaithfulness, the
    disloyalty, the violence and one of our biggest
    down falls 'the drug addiction's didn't know
And for that I apologize

I grew up in a dysfunctional alcoholic home
I was physically abused as a child and in a lot of
    pain from being sexually abuses as well
I acted out in anger and confusion and became
    a drug dealing stick up kid
At the age of sixteen years old with a gun in my hand making
    white people do what ever i told them to, it was power and
    control, even to this day i can't explain that feeling

I spent a lot of years in the state penitentiary
I lived like an animal and became a product of
    my environment so i acted like one to
I had know half way house, no were going to teach
    you how to be a good citizen class
I was just thrown back into society, i tried to become a productive
    citizen a good husband and father but i didn't have know
    tools to work with but what little knowledge i had
And i apologize

So i just became a ex convict ex drug addict, ex gang binger on
    public assistance with nothing but love and prayer to offer you,
And i apologize

As i grew older i grew wiser, and i didn't do know more stick
    ups and i try very hard not to do anything to jeopardize
    my freedom, i relapsed along the way making my own
    adjustments spending night after night out on the streets

were know one can find me in ally ways in crack houses and
   after a period of time it was know secret what i was doing
It may have been very embarrassing to you, or maybe a big
   let down because i was your first hero and i failed you
And i apologize

Because of my animalistic treating in prison and also from the
   fact that i am closiphobic I ended up with anxiety acts panic
   disorder and because of prison mixed with drug use bipolar
I may have said something's to you that has hurt your feelings,
   or done something's that you didn't understand
And i apologize

The fact is you have become a victim of my circumstances
And i apologize

Because of my incarcerations i wasn't there to protect you
When your mother boy friends neglected you
I wasn't there to teach you how to ride a bike fish
   and to celebrate all those birthdays misses
When i got out i tried to plat catch up, i tried, to fix all of those
   things i missed and i failed, it just didn't seem to be the same

I apologize for not being what was expected of me
You see i am also a victim of circumstances

I apologize for the times you had to be the man of
   the house, as a child because i wasn't there
I apologize for your mothers drug habit, even
   though she had it when i met her
I apologize for making you feel as though the
   street was more important then you
Were to me
I apologize for all of the parent and teacher meetings i missed
For not being they're when you took your first
   step or got your first report card
I apologize

I apologize for not having enough money to put you threw college
For not taking a stronger interest in you and your welfare

Dear son i can not fully explain to you why we go threw
        the things we go threw in life as black men.
I can't explain to you wy we must take these roads
        paved before us, but i can tell you this
God has a plan and a purpose for each and every one of us.
The only times we changed gods will is when we run off on our own
        and do what we want to do and not what God wants us to do
When we do that all we do is make our
        journey longer, and our way hard
Just to end up right were GOD wanted us in the first place

So if my actions have made your way troublesome in any way

'I apologize'

GET HIGH?
DIE?
WHY?
WHY MY BIG BROTHER BUBBA

One day we'll be in God's kingdom
Reminiscing about the past
All the good times we spent together
Just to get a laugh
I look forward to spending time with you
In our after life
Right now I'm gazing upon your tombstone
And I don't feel that nice
As my hopes for our heavenly gifts
Overcome my sorry
It gives me the strength to continue on
And make it to tomorrow
On one hand I wish you all the best
After all that we've been through
On the other hand I'm sad you're gone
Because I'm missing you
I gaze into the sky searching for your spirit
I call your name in my prayers, hoping you can hear it
Remember how we used to talk about when we grown up
How we will do the same
You will name your son after me
And I'll give my son your name
Remember when you taught me how to play basketball
And you kept blocking my shot
I still believe I could have won that game
You can believe it or not
Why did you start getting high man?
Why did you separate us?
You left me all alone
Just for a quick rush
Now what am I going to do

I can't believe you're gone
In my heart you will always live
In me you will live on
You could have come and talked with me
If you were having problems
Getting high just have you more
What? You thought that getting high would solve them?
I still have the last picture we took
Sitting on my dresser at home
But now the only thing I can picture
Is your name on a tombstone
Why did you start getting high man?
You didn't need that stuff
All the love you had in your life
Wasn't that enough
Now your poor children
Growing up without a dad
Most of the people at your funeral just shook their heads
And said, "Man, that's too bad".
Your mother outlived you
How do you think she feels?
When you got high, did you think it was OK?
"Boy, be for real"
One day we will be together again
In that great mansion beyond the sky
Then maybe you can explain to me, "Why?" "Big Brother"
"Why did you start getting high?"

ON THIS JOURNEY WE CALL LIFE

Life is not mystical to those who know how to submit to God
Man has tried many ways to stop the metamorphosis yet
We all must die. Would one rather be damned or dead
Or damned and alive, all living flesh becomes a corpse
Metamorphosis, life in the spirit and the spirit of men
Who knows the spirit of man, blood, mind and soul
The spirit of man, the tree of liberty is often
Fed with the blood of patriots and tyrants,
A fool and his money are soon parted
The best way to kill a race is to take away its ability to reproduce
Who's in prison? Sometimes nothing does so much
Harm as good intentions. To hope is to recognize
The possibility, so how can you know where I'm at
If you haven't been where I've been? Do you understand where
I'm coming from? A hateful man without reasons and accountability
Who is he? Life is yet a game and we are all players
Get your game tight, get a grasp on life and don't lose it
We all play different roles, we all have different goals and dreams
And yet we all move in one motion in the eyes of our God
While the politicians debate the people suffer
Democracy is not life, brings no happiness, life is within one's soul
A fool and his money are soon parted
Not everything you think is good for you, is good for you
Life is not mystical to those who understand living
To those who know how to live there's always a price to pay
'always' nothing matters as much as living
What is the use of legislation if we have no education
As we suffer, as we glory, we suffer, we kill each other
Yet call each other Brother living in strife
On the journey we call Life.

A VICIOUS CYCLE

Kicked out of the crack house and back in the street
I got no money, my body is hungry
And I ain't took a bath in about a week
My eyes are wide open and I'm on alert
On guard for my enemies cause I do dirt
Something in my head said, go to the shelter and stay
But I'm chasing my high and I got to get paid
Now I'm back on the drive through block
Where you can just drive up, roll your window down and cop um
Just standing on the corner full of hope
That the dealers don't catch me, a customer will
So I scratched my dirty ass and said, "man, I got to chill"
I've been in and out of jail all my life
I even contemplated suicide and rolled the death dice
Smoking don't make me a bad guy
I got it all under control and I can handle my high
My mother don't want me at her house
She told everyone I stole her VCR, man, she's got a big mouth
I'll go back to the shelter but it's too late
I'll go back to get some food but they already ate
What the hell am I going to do tonight
I'm tired of picking particles off the flour and to try and
Smoke it on my pipe
So business is bad and the night is slow
I'm kicked out of the crack house with no place to go
I look across the street at the corner store
If I can rob that place I won't be hungry no more
I robbed the store, I didn't take no food to eat
I just wanted to get high and keep running the street
With a pocketful of money I'm back at the crack house
Everyone's sitting around the table quiet as a church mouse
When I was broke they kicked me out, now they want me to stay
Someone will probably try to kill me if I try to walk away
So I just sat at the table and smoked
Rock after rock until I became broke

Kicked out of the crack house once again
Sweating, dirty and my body's stinking
The sun came up and it beamed bright
I'm weak because I've been up getting high all night
The shelter won't let me have a bed until five
And if I had one more hit, man, I can come alive
So I went back to the corner and I found
A car drive up with its window down
So I sold him some soap and sent him on his way
Now I'm back at the crack house welcome to stay
I had a couple of drinks and sex with a whore
Smoked up all my money and then they
    made me go back out the door
Just when I walked out of the house someone shot me
I thought I was too slick but they got me
Hit me in the back with a forty-five
The last words I heard was, "Is he alive -- Is he alive".
I woke up in the hospital, happy to be alive
Until the doctor came in and told me I've been paralyzed
I said to myself, "it just ain't fair"
First I'm kicked out of the crack house
Now I'm trapped in a wheel chair. A VICIOUS CYCLE.

FAST CHANGE GOT THE BEST OF ME

Fresh out of the joint with a brand new start
Back on the block, trying to make the best with what little I got
Filling out job applications but they're all denied
I have no history or experiences except for what I've done inside
I can pick up cigarette butts, stand up for count and watch TV
Well I did go to school, I got my GED
But these applications are asking for high school diplomas
Or a college degree
I can cook from a hot pot
And make a good cup of Kool Aid
I can also go back to my old block, pump dope and get paid
But I left jail telling myself I'm going to succeed
Yah, life is what you make it but nothing is guaranteed
Thank God I saved up enough money in jail to get my own crib
But next month when I can't pay rent, then where will I live?
I can find me a girl that's on welfare and move into her place
But I want a brand new start, not another
     rate race in someone else's space
My back's against the ropes and I'm losing the fight
Between a rock and a hard place and only I want to do what's right
A man's got to do what he must to survive
I should have just faced reality instead I fantasized
Thinking I can make it in a world of constant stereotype
Where I can't trust no man, whether black or white
All I need is a job to earn an honest pay
But they just look at me, shake their head and slowly walk away
The same man that did my drugs and tricked off with my whores
Won't trust me enough to give me a job, clean
     windows or open his doors
So I did all I could cause I've been all I can be
I'm back on the block, punching my clock
Dealing dope, will I get caught, I hope I don't
Cause fast change ain't no robbery
It is cool to flip burgers and shake fries
And believe the lies

Or is it cool to pay my rent, dress slick
Drive my cars, BMWs and Jaguars
I do what I have to, to survive
Fast change ain't no robbery
But it will always get the best of me without a clue
I'm back in the courtrooms but I did what I had to do
Am I a victim of circumstance
Or a man who never had a chance
So I sit here in the courthouse gazing at 12 people ready to judge me
Most likely I'll be found guilty
Then the judge will determine whether to lock me up or set me free
Yet, no one was there when I couldn't find a job
No one was there when I was praying to God
To bless me with money so I can eat
And to give me the strength to make it to the street
No one was there when I sung the blues
Walking in the snow with holes in my shoes
No one was there when I shed my tears
I've been hated and rejected, for years and years
No one was there when I cried out for help
Fast change ain't no robbery, but it what is its result?
Am I a victim of circumstance, a reject of society?
Fast change ain't no robbery, but it always got the best of me
I'm sitting in my jail cell facing a lot of time
Lonely, confused and mad
With vengeance on my mind
Teardrop don't come down because my heart is to hard to cry
My willpower is too strong to hang myself and die
So who commits the crimes and who is really free
Is your politics and traditions reality or robbery
Does this system that you set up help the rich and the poor
Or does the rich keep getting richer and the poor die in war?
You're a thief and I'm a thief, let's face reality
You rob, steal and kill politically
And the fast change I make to savor, it ain't no robbery
I'm not guilty, not as society
Fast change ain't no robbery

Yet it always got the best of me, it always got the best of me.

Trust and betrayal
Passion or conspiracy
Reality and robbery
Need or greed
Everyone will like to succeed
Yah, life is what you make it
But nothing is guaranteed -- but robbery
It always got the best of me
Looking for change in society.

Enjoying My Family
In a
Peaceful Way

I woke this morning in a peaceful way
Said my prayers, had a coffee, and started
Off my day

Got into my car and started off to work
Someone had road rage flipped me the finger
And called me a jerk

I broke down on the highway with a broken fan belt
For two hours I sat there waiting for some help
So I walked two miles to a gas station
They didn't believe me when I explained
My situation

Finally I got a tow truck to take me on my way
They wanted to see my ID to make sure I
Wasn't stealing someone else's triple A

I got my car fixed and started off again
And then I got pulled over by a police man

He wanted to know what I was doing in that neighborhood
Treated me like a thief that was
Up to no good

He gave me a sobriety test
Put me in hand cuffs like I was under arrest

He called my name in for warrants and then let
Me go
Then he warned me to be cautious and drive slow

I stopped at the store for some chewing gum
Everyone was staring at me
Like I had a gun
Security was following me around the store
Like I was the enemy, and we was in a silent war

Finally I made it to work, late for the first time
My boss is screaming and was going out of his mind

Threatened to fire me if I was late again
And this is when all my problems at work begin

Some co-workers act high sidity
Others are just raunchy
And two-faced, and to damn pretty

Some smile in your face, and stab you in the back
Some don't say nothing cause they don't like blacks
Some are soft and understanding
And some are just too hard
I want to pack up and quit,
But I need this job

Because times are hard
My boss is crazy
The guy that works with me is so damn lazy
He sits around all day drinking coffee and tea
Thinking all the work should be done by me

I got a house full of kids
I need food for the fridge
I got a lot of bills to pay
So I held my pride and made
It through the day

I went home to my wife and kids
And looking at there faces, gives me the strength
To live
In a world thats corrupt, and full of so much stress
We still have each other, never the less
And in spite of all my problems
I finished my day
Enjoying my family
In a peaceful way

I WAS ONCE BLIND
BUT NOW I SEE
THE FUTURE LOOKS GOOD FOR EVERY MAN

Looking at life through the eyes of a child
With faith and joy and a gentle smile
But as I grow older and become a man
The racism, the hate, I could never understand
Discrimination and segregation, society and racial tension
The white house war against the poor
Republicans, blacks and Christians
I once was blind but now I see
Private prisoners, house maids, and home slaves
Fire, brimstone and the horrors of hell
Descendents of slaves, the violence and silence
And things we were made never to tell
Walking in darkness seeking the light
Mississippi River lead me on
Beyond the sorrow, hate and death
Beyond the plantation where I was born
I can see the trails of blood from Washington, DC
The lynching and tension in Memphis, TN
The Birmingham scam
The raping and hating in slavery
The things we were robbed of
The things we were giving
The will power that kept us wanting to keep living
The tragic mistakes and violent outbreaks
We still stand with pride and loyalty of kings
In broken slave chains and poor people's campaigns
The demand is high to pioneer another coalition
To organize a committee particularly
For those who are blind and for those who will still listen
I once was blind but now I see
The land of the rich, the land of the free
And the foolish scams you've played on me

Held down by political conspiracy
Ruler of darkness and powerful liars
With hidden tactics to create invisible chains
To hold us back and keep us struggling
Like pieces in a chess game
From Queen Elizabeth to King James
From the white house castle
To the smallest pawn
You will be conquered
And life will go on
So the revolution "will be" televised
When the world sees through your foolish lies
And all your social organizations of bigotry
Will come tumbling down
Like a Mississippi Valley
What the devil means for bad, God means for good
One day we will all understand
I once was blind, but now I see
The future looks good for every man.

Fortunate

Once upon a time
There was a wise warrior
Who found a horse
And everyone said how fortunate he was

Then one day the horse threw him off
And he broke both of his legs
And everyone said how
Unfortunate he was

Then there was a great battle
And everybody died
Expect for the wise warrior
Who couldn't go because he
Broke his leg

EXPRESSION OF RESPECT

TODAYS YOUTH ARE TOMORROW ADULTS
IF CRIME INCREASE,WE CAN'T LIVE IN PEACE
AND THOSE WILL BE THE RESULTS
OF TODAY'S ADULTS NOT TAKING A STAND
TO LEAD THE YOUTH, WITH A LOVING HAND
IT TAKES A VILLAGE, A COMMUNITY AND THE
BECOME WON YOUTH PROGRAM
TO TEACH THE YOUTH TO EXPRESS THEIRSELF
WITH LOVE AND RESPECT
TO TEACH THEM TO VALUE LIFE WITH
KNOWLEDGE THEY'LL NEVER FORGET
TO BRIDGE ENDLESS COMMUNITY OPPRESSION
WITH POETRY AND PLAY,
TO MENTOR EDUCATE AND WIN OUR
NEIGHBORHOODS
AND HELP THEM GET GOOD GRADES
SO WE ARE THE BECOME WON YOUTH PROGRAM
AND THIS IS WHAT WE DO
WE MENTOR EDUCATE AND THEACH THE YOUTH
TO RESPECT LIFE'S GREAT VALUES

Never Give Up

There was two mice that fell in
A bucket of cream, swimming to stay alive
One gave up and died
The other kept trying until
The cream turned into butter
And then he just walked out

Pot of Gold

There were two trees in the garden
One of good and evil, the other of life
If eating your fruit is evil
Then I've got to make a sacrifice
You're the apple of my eyes
The yam of my sweet desire
The avocado of my flow
The nut that lights my fire
The nectarine of my fondest dreams
And you artichoke when I stroke
Cause I'm long, like a rainbow
Strong like a tree
There's no harm in
Being in your garden
Another sweet memory
And also I want you to know
Good things do come to pass
I pray you do
Let me hold onto you
My pot of gold at last.

My Hood Incognito

I wear my hoody no my head, incognito
Scourged in a world that treats me unequal
I'm just a product of the society you made
With the hopes and dreams of getting paid

I wear my hoody on my head

I wear my hoody on my head in remembrance of the confusion
I had all my childhood which started me to using
Drugs to escape my unfair abusive painful space,
    so I can escape to another place

A drug addict struggling everyday
To stay clean and live a better way,

Follow the lead of your leader, live by example they said
I have no leaders; see all my leaders are dead

So your give me the president of this rich country instead
Other countries children starving, children dead
He sits in the white house drinking wine and breaking bread
And I'm having a hard time making sure my own children are fed
And just to escape the confusion of this dysfunctional world

I wear my hoody on my head

I wear my hoody on my head, because I'm feeling the pain
I have enough since in my brain to know that
    we're not being treated the same
And most of my people, don't know whether they're
    coming or going or from where they came

The night life is the right life for the street thug
Everyone is under some mind altering, mood changing drug
The prisons are filled over it's capacity
And 90% of the inmates look like me
With the hopes and dreams of being free
And for the sisters raising the families
Alone at home
Not knowing if daddy is alive or dead

I wear my hoody on my head

I wear my hoody on my head because I've been holding a grudge
Playing the blame game and associating with those who show no love
So the only one I hurt is me
Scourged in a world that treats me in everyway but equal
So I live incognito
Material things don't bring true wealth
No one could put a price on good health
Feel me as I express myself

I took my hoody off

I took my hoody off to look up at the sky
I had my head down so long I didn't realize
How beautiful are the shapes of the clouds
The sunshine and the color blue
The changing of the seasons and the way people do
See some things just happen because God allows them to

I took my hoody off, and put on a suit and tie
Fill out a job application without telling a lie
The hood never allowed me to see
The reality, the beauty, the man that I can truly be
So I played the hand life dealt to me

I took my hoody off

I took my hoody off, lift my chin and stood like a man
If the next man can succeed, then this man can
Change is good out of the hood

As long as it's done in a positive way
See life is not a game, and Russian roulette is fools play
Yes the night life is the right life for those who are lost
So the next time you ask someone what's up," look up"wiseup"
AND TAKE YOUR HOODY OFF
I wear my hoody incognito

Love & Hate

Out of the abundance of the heart the mouth speaks. Peter 1:
23 says: For you have been born again, not of the perishable
seen but of the imperishable through the "living" and enduring
God. Do you love the Lord? Do you "love" the Lord with your
heart, mind and soul? Are you a good seen sown on good soil?
YOU CAN'T LOVE THE LORD AND HATE YOUR BROTHER
Ex 20:6 Mt 22:38 Jn 13:34 These are just a few scriptures where
God's commandments are that we "love" each other and "love"
the Lord and the "keep" his commandments. Come out of the
darkness and into the light. Put on the whole armor of God, don't
just half dress. You won't leave your house with a shirt and shoes
and not have on your pants or underwear; you will look real funny
walking around like that. In fact you will probably get arrested.
And having done all to stand, then stand fully dressed! My sons
do not know how I used to be as a child, but I look at them and
their ways and see myself. We are children of God and we must
have God's ways. When people look at you, what do they see?

> We serve a forgiving God.
> We serve a humble God.
> We serve a God of authority and power.
> We serve a God of holiness and righteousness.
> We serve a God of courage and wisdom.
> We serve a God of joy and grace.
> We serve a God of freedom and strength.
> We serve a God of knowledge and splendor.
> We serve a God of "love".
> And only through his mercy are we saved.

And Lord have mercy on your souls because he hears when you talk
about each other. He knows your thoughts. We have brothers and
sisters in the church doing right with the church and God. They
take part in the church activities, helping with the children, take tie
to clean the church, just giving God their all. And here you come,
you used to come to church two and three times a week but now
since the lord has blessed you with a good job and a new car, you

don't have to depend on another brother or sister to pick you up and take you to church, you start slacking. You just got a new VCR and there is a movie you want to see "every" Saturday night and you just don't have it in you to get up and get the kids ready and make it to church. So now you just show up every now and then, or you have a man or woman living with you and you don't want the church to know. When you do show up, all you do is look down on those who are less fortunate than you are and all you do with your walk is complain to the pastor. Because you have been coming to church since you were a child, in fact your mother and father grew up in church and how come you can't teach Sunday school or be a choice director or an usher, like sister so and so, whose only been coming to church for a year. Out of your ignorance and jealous behavior, you start talking about such and such, every chance you get, prejudging, misjudging, and by your own judgment you condemn yourself. I am not only talking to the women, you men know what I am talking about too. You even go as far as to find others in the church with the same evil spirit. And after talking about sister such and such like a dog, you all decide to get together and counsel sister such and such, trying to get the speck out of her eye when you got a plank in your own eye. How do you take the plan out of your eye? Ask the Lord for forgiveness. Turn from your backyard before you go talking about how dirty someone else's backyard is.

Is it bad enough that the world is constantly misjudging Christians. If you don't believe me, put on a T-shirt that has lettering on front and back "For Christ I live and For Christ I Will Die". Wear this to your next family cookout or family gathering. Leave a tape recorder on the table and record. Walk away slowly with this scripture on your back and see how many people slander you, talk about you like a dog and as soon as you come back, you will see that the one's that talked about you the most will be the first one to smile in your face and act like they would never do such a thing behind your back. Just because you live for Jesus and you have come out of the world and do not fit in with the world and its lust anymore, some will see the change and hate on you. You will be the big event of the day, the main attraction. I have been locked up in prison and persecuted, insulted, living in a closet with hundreds of worldly men and had all kinds of false rumors spreading about me. If it was not for the spirit of the Lord teaching me the Beatitudes, I might have given up on the Christian walk a long time ago. If you go back to Matthew 5:11 you will read the word BLESSED in big letters. Blessed are you "yes you are". Count your blessing and know that you are blessed. Blessed are you when people in church and on the streets insult you, persecute you and falsely say all kinds of evil against you. Yes, it is evil, it is down right evil. All kinds of evil against you are because of me, said the Lord. Do not take it personal, we are in a war, a spiritual war, for we fight not against flesh and blood but against principalities and darkness. That means we fight against the rulers, against the authorities, against the powers of this dark world, against the spiritual forces of evil, against evil, evil in heavenly places, yes, even in church.

But Math 5:12 says *"Rejoice, Rejoice and be glad, because great is your reward in heaven, for in the same way, they persecuted the Prophets which were before you."*

Paul and John the Baptist were beheaded. John, the brother of James, was exiled to the Island of Patmos. (In fact, they tried to kill John by putting him in boiling oil, but the oil would not touch him so they called him a witch and kicked him out.) Peter was crucified upside down. Back then they took Christians and put them in prison and tormented them from the Old to the New Testament Christians have been persecuted. Did you know that most of the Bible was written by inspired Christians that were in prison, in chains, locked down. Yes, most of the Bible was written in prison. And some churches won't even let you in to preach if you're supporting the prison ministry. Satan and his wicked ways don't have the victory, in the name of Jesus, we got Him.

David wrote about his struggles in the Psalms. In fact, when he wrote Psalm 59, Saul was sending men to David's house to kill him. David ran to the house of Ahimelech, the Palestinians seized him in Gath. He fled from Saul into a cave. They were

trying to destroy David and it was when Saul sent me to
watch David's house to kill him when he wrote Psalm 59:

> Deliver me from my enemies O God
> Protect me from those who rise up against me
> Deliver me from evil doers
> And save me from blood thirsty men
> See how they lie and wait for me like dogs
> Fierce men conspire against me
> Arise to help me, look on my plight
> O Lord God Almighty, the God of Israel
> Rouse yourself to punish the nations
> Show no mercy to wicked traitors

He called them wicked traitors. People who smile in your face,
all the time they want to take your place. There are backstabbers
even in the church, yes, they're in the church too. They pray
with you with one hand and stab you in the back with the other
one, talk about you like a dog. They return at evening snarling
like dogs, yes, like dogs and prowl about the city. See what the
spew from their mouths, they spew out swords from their lips.

The Bible says: It is not what goes in the mouth that defiles
the body but what comes out of it. Yes, words can kill and
cause great harm. There's power in words. The devil takes
what we say and runs with it and we give him ammunition
to shoot other people down. But the word of God is might
and no weapon formed against you shall prosper. But:

> Blessed are the poor in spirit
> Blessed are those who morn
> Blessed are the meek
> Blessed are those who hunger for righteousness
> Blessed are the merciful
> Blessed are the pure in heart
> Blessed are the peacemakers
> Blessed are the persecuted for righteousness sake.

And blessed are "YOU" when people insult you, when people persecute you, when people falsely say all kinds of evil against you because you love the Lord for the Lord's sake, because you sow seeds and pay tithes, because you are not ashamed of the Gospel of Christ and its power, because for Christ you will live and for Christ you will die, because you give 99.9% of yourself to Jesus, because you are what you say you are "Born Again", a new creation, because all things work together for good to those that love the Lord, to those who are called according to purpose. Rejoice and be glad because "great" is your reward in heaven.

He goes on to say in chapter seven, verse six:
> Do not give *dogs* what is sacred, yes, dogs
> Do not throw your pearls to *pigs*, yes, pigs
> If you do they will trample them under their feet
> And then turn and tear you to pieces
> Don't give the devil a foothold
> And don't give him any ammunition
> And first and foremost, *DO NOT JUDGE* or
> You will be judged
> In the same way you judge and with the measure you use
> It will be measured to you.
> And you a dog? Then don't live like one.
> Are you a pig? Then don't carry yourself like one.

BE HOLY – BE BLESSED – BE LIKE 'JESUS'

REST IN PEACE

A part of me, now gone
And I'm missing you
A part of me, gone to heaven
And I'm missing you
So I sing this song for you
Have a talk with God for me
Live my love in heaven above
Farewell, rest in peace.

A part of me, a part of you
Never apart
A part of you
Will always be
Here, in my heart
So I sing this song for you
As a prayer to God from me
After all the love from heaven above
Farwell, rest in peace.

Everyone's born to live
Everyone sees itthrough
Within this world
Of love and hate
We die
Because we do
Everyone's born to live
I wonder when will be my day
I'll live my life and struggle through
I will not go astray.

Continued

I'll help to feed the hungry
And brighten up the sad
Do helpful things in life, indeed
For those who never had
It often brings me sorrow
And fills my heart with pain
To see loved ones with crying eyes
Their tears fall like rain
Now that you're gone I'm lonely
Can you see it in my eyes
I see it each and every day
I wonder, I wonder why.

Everyone has to go
Everyone sees it through
Within this world
Of love and hate
We die
Because we do.

After all the love you gave
After all the peace at least
Live happy my love in heaven above
Good bye
Rest in peace
I will see you again my friend
Rest in peace.....

I'VE GOT INSURANCE

I opened my mailbox
And what did I see
Another letter for life insurance
This one was addressed to me
I read that I can be insured for a small monthly fee
So I got my pen and paper
And I wrote that company

I've got insurance
Jesus Christ
I pay no monthly fee
I've got insurance
Jesus Christ paid the price with his life for me

You can depend on mankind
Or depend on God
Once you give your life to Jesus
You don't need any special card

I've got the truth of God
And righteousness I claim
The gospel of peace, the shield of faith, helmet of salvation
The sword of the spirit
And the victory in Jesus' name
I've got insurance
I pay no monthly fee
I've got insurance
Jesus Christ paid the price with his life for me.

SALVATION

To whom it may concern:

My name is Sinner Man
And I'd like to change it to Saint
I was told I had to come to you first
I know we never met before
But I've heard a lot about you
See I've had this name all of my life
And I'm afraid to go on without you
My Ma told me she prayed for me
My Grandma told me you paid for me
I was never a man of wealth
I've struggled every day
A debt that I could never pay
I struggled every day.

Dear Lord, hear my cry
I don't want to be a Sinner Man no more
Especially when I die
Can I come to you when life gets me down
Would you be my friend
On an unmeasured scale
Body for body, pound for pound
Forever yours.

SAINT
My letter from Jesus
My dear child Saint
Romans 3:23
Romans 6:23
Sincerely yours, *Jesus Christ*

MY SHADOW, MY SON

I see you following me
Doing the things that I do
Science would say it's impossible
For me to follow you
There's light within your mist
We can't go on without the light
Living in a wicked world
Living in darkness
Travel with me, move within motion
Feel the vibrations, sense my emotion
Speak to me, I know you know
Follow me, feel my soul
There you are wherever I go
Me and my shadow
Me and my shadow
One times one plus one
The only one that's true
The only one I trust
One times ones, is one, plus one, is two
Who else besides me, besides my shadow
My son.

A SPECIAL DAY
YOUR FIRST DAY ON EARTH

Today is a special day
For me as well as you
Nature seems to bless us
Everyday with something new
Today is a new beginning
To some it's an end
Someone made an enemy
Someone made a friend
Some will be on time
And some will show up late
So call your friends and enemies
It's time to celebrate
Bake a cake, blow out the candles
Have a drink and laugh
Because today is the day
The doctor slapped your ass
I know this may sound violent
But what else can I say
I thought it was lame
To just sign my name
And say "Happy Birthday"
When I can remind you of the pain
You first received birth
I'm not your enemy
You're more than a friend to me
Let's celebrate
Your first day on earth.

REMINDED BY A RAINBOW

I've heard many songs
I've read many poems
My sunshine and my storms
This morning was kind of dreary
As I gazed upon the dew
And then I saw a rainbow
That's when I thought of you.

Your eyes are like the stars
As they glitter through the night
Your teeth are like the clouds
So pure and pearly white
Your love reminds me of the sky
So strong, so soft, so blue
And when I see a rainbow
I'll always think of you.

LAST NIGHT I'VE LIED

At night I close my eyes
And dream about you
Reality awakes me
Most dreams don't come true
And then I fantasize
And use my imagination
Some may say that I'm a dreamer
And you're just a hallucination
I pray to see your face
And I love your personality
Could you just be a dream
Should I just face reality
My heart has been broken
And I'm not ashamed to say
I'm afraid to get close to you
Cause you might walk away
I like the sound of your voice
And that little giggle that you do
I may not be in love yet
But I might have a crush on you
Because at night when I close my eyes
No matter how hard I try
I tell myself I'm not going to dream about you
But again, last night, I've lied.

179

FOREVER, SINCERELY TRUE, I DO

You introduced me as a friend
And oh, how I want to be more
Than just a friend to you
Always and forever
Sincerely true I do
I truly want you to know
How much I yearn to be with you
With all the love from heaven above
I present myself sincere and true
I dedicate my life to you
To fulfill your every need
Through sickness and health
I surrender myself
Lifetime guaranteed
Thinking of you with someone else
Just fills my heart with pain
Jealousy, envy, strife, brokenness and shame
I know that you're a good woman
I hurt when others do you wrong
The pain I've watched you go through
You handled, held on and stayed strong

Continued

I love to touch your skin
And look into your eyes
I like to watch you walk
Oh, how I fantasize
I yearn to be your man
More than words can ever say
Me and you forever girl
Forever that's what I pray
I'm way past the stage of playing mind games
And too caring to be inconsiderate
I want more for you, I truly do
Than to just go through
A platonic relationship
I want you to be my woman
Conquer the world
Me and you
I want you to be with me forever
Sincerely true, I do.

AS MUCH AS I LOVE YOU

Oh, how I miss you
Words could not express
How I wish to be with you
To me you are the best
Warmest thoughts are with you
As you go through your day
Special thoughts that wish you more
Than words could ever say
Warmest thoughts are with you
In everything you do
Because there is no one else
Who loves you like I do
I've heard many songs sung
I've read many poems
I've had life's problems
My sunshine and my storms
I've met many people
Even fell in love with one or two
But I've never loved anyone
As much as I love you.

FEELINGS OF COMPASSION

Relying on relationships
And dealing with friends
Feelings of compassion for my companions
If I was to fall in love with you I'll have to make amends
And tell my lover I found another, relying on a friend
Trying to love two is very hard to do
And I sacrificed my life to fall in love with you
Did you ever love someone but she didn't care
Did you ever feel like crying but knew you'll get nowhere
Did you ever fall in love with someone your lover knew
You tried so had to tell someone but just did not know how to
When we talk and I hear your voice, it warms me up inside
And now out loud, I say it proud, I have nothing to hide
I love you more than you can know, deep down in my heart
If you say yes, I'll tell my ex, and no one will pull us apart
I know this may be shocking news to you
We were friends, good companions
And what else can I do
Because I do really love you
Maybe the word love is a little strong
And we haven't talked about this very long
But my emotions seem to always get the best of me
And when I talk about you, love won't let me be
This has got to be the saddest day in my life you know
Because I have to make this choice and let someone go
Although we have had our good times, yes it's true
And right now even you may not know what to do
Just let your heart be your guide
Because if you use your head, you may manipulate yourself
And later on find out you lied, and make a bad choice instead
Times a wastin' and the future is no guarantee
Rely on our relationship
And let your feelings free.

YOU MAKE ME WANNA LEAVE THE ONE I'M WITH

You make me want to
Leave the one I'm with
And start a new relationship
With you.
Life is full of choices
And there's always a choice
Why drive a Chevrolet
When I can drive a Rolls Royce
Why smell a dandelion
When I can sniff a rose
Why wear hand me downs
When I can wear brand new clothes
Why work in a factory
When I can sit behind my own des
Why should I be with the one I'm with
If I'm just settling for less
Life is made of choices
And I've got to do
What I've got to do
'cause you make me wanna leave the one I'm with
And start a new relationship with you.

Continued

Life is full of choices
And I've made my choice
I saw doves fly
When I first heard your voice
When I think about you I don't know why
My heart tingles inside my chest
And when I think about the one I'm with
I see I've been settling for second best
So I am to tell her our relationship is through
Because you make me want leave the one I'm with
And start a new relationship with you
Cupid must have shot me right in my ass
How do I know, because I can't let go
And I love to hear your laugh
I even told my mom, how good you make me feel
Like riding in a rose
In brand new clothes
With love behind the wheel
You make me wanna jump into the sky
And live on cloud nine
You make me wanna show the whole world
"look y'all, ain't she fine"
You make me wanna give up the world
And dedicate my life to you
You make me wanna do all kinds of things
I normally wouldn't do
You make me wanna hop, jump and skip, even back flip
Leave the one I'm with
And start a new relationship with you.

MY LITTLE CHOCOLATE QUEEN

I fell in love with a black woman
Young and full of dreams
To raise a family in a functional home
Me and my chocolate queen
One day we will say our vows
Till death do us part
Through sickness and health
Poor or good wealth
Happy or sad
Good and bad
That's when my problems started
As long as I made money
She was by my side
But when I went to jail she melted
So did my chocolate pride
Living well above my means
To satisfy my little queen
I broke the law and went to jail
Now I'm in and she is out
And I can't make my bail
I dressed her in gold
And designer clothes
Driving foreign cars
People would gloat and hold their heart
Like we were superstars
What's mine was hers
What's hers was hers
With greed and selfishness
My home boys called me pussy whipped
Because I lived like this
Now I'm in jail masturbating, thinking of the past
Of when I see my chocolate queen
So she can kiss my ass
So she can melt as a result
And slowly fade away
'cause I'm the nut that don't give up
I'll live another day

BLACK WOMEN RISE
BE STRONG AND SURVIVE

Life is a death trap, where only the strong can survive
Remember politics and Watergate, stealing and selling lies
Having the best in life is nothing if it brings out the worst in you
S how can you sit and judge me when you do the same things I do?
A lawyer gets caught for embezzlement
A DA gets busted taking bribes
Police are out getting high
And the FBI are steadily telling lies
And stands a young brother like me
With a dream to be all I an be
But afraid to fall in love
'cause I might not land on my feet
Black women I know, life is hard
And rent is always short
Your man's in jail but he knows how you feel
We all can use a little support
He dreams of making love to you
To have all of you to himself
While he fantasizes about you in his mind
You're making love to someone else
Don't kick to the curb
And leave him in the street
He's not a cat so don't throw him like that
'cause he might not land on his feet

Continued

Remember the times of old when we were loyal till death did us part
From the cotton field to the slop we ate, yet nothing broke our hearts
Are you so brain washed, mentally lost, watered down the weak
To take a man to court for child support
With a restraining order to keep him in the street
We once ran from the slave man, didn't know
	where we was going but made it here
Now you run to the slave man from me, claiming to be in fear
Life is a death trap, where only the strong can survive
I don't say this to put you down
But to open your eyes to realize
A farmer's best crop is fertilized in the best shit
And we've had our shit in life
Black woman, my queen, I pray that we can rise again
And stop calling me a nigger, acting like the slave man
So many people got lynched and hung for
	the things we take for granted
Some committed suicide cause they just couldn't stand it
Stand by your man black woman and he will stand by you
And once you start to count your blessings you
	will se that dreams do come true
I got calluses on my hands, pain in my heart and fire in my eyes
We've been through a lot but only the strong can survive
Black women, I know life is hard
You take care of your children and pray to God
You need a man standing firm on his own
Someone you can call the head of the home
Ignorance comes in all nationalities
And close friends can be the worst enemies
We all got the world on our back
We just suffer cause we're black

Continued

And if a man had a woman's support
We can overcome that 'fact'
Black women, stand on your feet
I know it's had on the street
Living in danger ain't no game
A young black man in a casket, such a shame
Who's gonna pay for his tombstone
A young black mother broke and all alone
They're sending people to the moon, that's good
But they can't keep drugs out of the neighborhood
Black women, open your eyes, watch the sun rise
And realize, use your head and be wise
Cause only the strong can survive
Never be ashamed of what you are
And always be all you can be
But you can't be all that
Unless you be with me
Cause I'm a young black man making it
Not like the man who's faking it
Life is hard and I hate it
But only the strong can survive.

SPECIAL FRIENDS

I'm not perfect girl, I know
And there have been times
When you could have let me go
I know I've troubled you in the past
When all your associates said "Leave his ass!"
But you had a vision for you and me
At one time I couldn't see
The dreams you wanted to fulfill
If I knew I would have chilled
Well, maybe not, but now I know
Why you never let me go
A bird lays its eggs with joyful pride
The trees proudly praise the sky
I wish there was more I could do
Than be a special friend to you
You show me love with great devotion
Never did you have mixed emotions
In times of trouble and times of need
Your friendship was always guaranteed
To show me love and see me through
I always had a friend in you
You have shown me beyond degree
With peace and grace and unity.

DESTRUCTION

Title
Uncleanness-Depression-Discouragement-Defeat-
    Jealousy-Criticism-Judgement-Destruction

Text
Matthew 12:43-45

Introduction
Jesus told the story of a "man" who had gotten saved.
He also talked about how the devil
Had to get out when the man got saved
I call this man, "BLACK MAN"

If we could pull the curtain back and see beyond
The physical realm. We will witness the diabolical scene.
Picture if you will....

The unclean spirit goes to a convention of demons
He has found no rest outside of Black Man
The body of which he once lived in
The unclean spirit tries to sneak out of the convention
As Lucifer stands screaming at the demons
Flaming fingers in his direction, fiery arrows
Aimed at the demons
Satan says "What are you doing here, Uclean?"
"I thought I sent you to possess Black Man?"
"Give me an account of yourself
It better be good".
Now every wicked spirit is looking at Unclean
As he shakes with fear and speaks with a
Trembling voice
I was living in Black Man for years
I had him doing drugs, lying, stealing

Continued

And doing every unclean thing I made him do
Until Sunday when he went to church in prison
And accepted Jesus into his heart
Satan yells with a violent rage until all Hell shakes
"Don't ever say that name again in my presence
I hate it, I hate it"
As the brimstone walls glow with reflected fire
Another demon stands up
My name is "Discouragement" I will go with
Unclean to visit Black Man. I will work a
Few things to make him Discouraged.
I'll just have someone from his church to go
The new pastor and say nasty things about him.
Another demon stands to speak
My name is "Depression", I'll go with Unclean and
Discouragement. I'll make him feel as if he is
Not wanted in the church because he's black and
I'll make him feel less than depressed.
A third demon stands, my name is "Defeat"
I've worked a lot of churches and people like Black Man.
I'll go when things are at a low point
I'll take a brother from the church who works
With him on his job and have him snitching
Other people out and lying on others for a very
Small raise. When Black Man sees this he will
Leave the job, church and be defeated.
Excitement is starting to build.
The fourth demon jumps to his feet and claps
His hands with glee.

Continued

My name is "Jealousy", when Discouragement, Depression
And Defeat go with Unclean, let me go too.
When Black Man gets really defeated and starts
Taking a look around the church
I'll show him all of the back stabbing snitches
Who make more trouble than disciple's in the church
Those who would do anything to be choir director or
Guitar player. I'll have him looking at other
People instead of the Word of God.
I'll have him complaining about the position in the church
That other people who have not even been
Called by God or anointed by God
'I'll make him so jealous he won't ever get over it
The fifth demon jumps up. My name is "Criticism"
And I want to go.
I'll get him to start criticizing just a little bit
With just a little sarcasm.
Pretty soon he'll be attacking everybody
Of course, I'll make sure some people criticize
Him too.
What's good for sin is good for the sinner
The sixth demon stands to offer his services
I'm the spirit of "Judgement"
After Black Man has been overcome by criticism
I'll cause him to start passing judgement on them
Like never before
I'll even make him say the whole church are nothing
But hypocrites
And they need to go straight to where we are if you
Know what I mean?
Finally a big sour looking demon pulls himself
Up into a hateful, steady, seasoned voice
He begins to speak

Continued

My name is "Destruction"
The plan of action against Black Man sounds
Good to me.
I would like to give the final touch
Just as he starts to lack faith in that guy in that
Book. That we killed on the cross and came back to life.
I'll hit Black Man with RACISM.
I'll remind him how much people don't like him and
How many people died because of the color of their skin
Then I'll let him know that his cultural Christian
Values are different than the other leaders in the church
I'll also make him believe that the church is segregating
Against blacks and he can't do anything about it
I'll remind him that he had an all white jury in court
And racism is something he can't escape, not even in
His church.
I'll make him get high on drugs in order not to face
His thoughts of destruction.
I'll have him "No Way Out", a place to call home
I'll have his wife leave him and break contact with his family
I'll take away his parole so he can just give up on the
One he used to praise
I'll give him a TV to watch on Sunday mornings
This will keep him in his cell and out of church
I'm the last resort for these other six demons
You might say. I'm the straw that breaks the camels back.
I'm the head of Satan's tormenting spirits (Uncleanness-
Depression-Discouragement-Defeat-Jealousy-Criticism-
Judgment). My name is DESTRUCTION.

WHERE ARE YOU NOW?

Everything has its season, its order
There's nothing new under the sun
A child is born and somebody dies
What is your natural state of mind?
Good and evil?
Everything has its order
As nature takes its course
Life goes on
Who am I to question the universal power
Of its almighty repetitive order
People die because people live
The planet is only so big
So we live, so we die
What is my soul? Do I have a unique spirit?
Is there any reincarnation?
Is there a heavenly waiting place?
Everything has its order
Where did I come from?
Who is good, who is evil?
What is your state of mind?
I'm searching for a reason
Why did you have to die?
Why were you taken away?
Where did you go?
Where are you now?

SUPERIOR COURT RECORD

Living in a fantasy
Man, I had more drugs than the pharmacy
Where are you from kid? You don't know me?
Man, you can ask anybody
You don't want to be my enemy
Boy, *you better check my record*
Living in a fantasy.
Crack on me about the clothes I'm in?
I'm not from the tennis shoes generation
I used to flaws in slacks gators and snake skin
And stay sharp as a 'hat pin'
Boy, *you better check my record*
Living in a fantasy.
My rep alone holds its own
All my life I've been a stick up kid
And I ain't going back to do another bid
And if they ask who did it, I'm gonna say "I did"
You better check my record
Living in a fantasy.
I stay 'strapped', 'strong', I roll deep
Next time the police pull up on me
I'm gonna hold court right here on the street
And if I jack you, kid, you just got beat
Boy, *you better check my record*
Living in a fantasy.
Hardwear, I got heavy gear
Live or die, man, I don't care
Boy, *you better check my record.*

Continued

Reality awakes me
It was one hot summer day
Drama came my way
Frustrated as I can be
I said, boy, you don't know me
He pulled out his jamy, I turned around
And my boys left me standing alone
So I'm looking around on the ground
Like a dog looking for a bone
Bullets started to fly
And so did I
I didn't rob that kid
Someone else did
Now I'm in the courtroom

Facing a long bit
Reality awakes me
Just been found guilty by a 12 man jury
The judge is about to sentence me
Lock me up or set me free
I 'begged' my lawyer
Man, let me take the stand
Cause no one can plead my case
The way I can
So I took the stand
At first my story was being accepted
My lawyer was expensive and well respected
Then all of a sudden every call he made was cut off, or disconnected
Even my revise or revoke was rejected
I said "Your Honor, why?"
He said "Son, you're going to prison
Just as the court expected
When you took the stand
We checked your record".
Long records get no support in *superior court*
I checked your record.

THE WORLD IS YOURS

It's important that young black men check
Their history and have a good understanding of self
Who they are, Where they are
How they got here and where they would like to go
Have a good understanding of God
Gods will and self, Gods will for self
If you can crawl, you can walk
If you can walk, you can run
As long as the rivers run
And the earth is by the rain and the sun
As long as the stars shine from the heavens
As long as the rivers run to the sea
You can be whatever you wish to be
You came too far in life and history
Run and faint not
If you want success
All you need to do is
:succeed"
The world is yours.

DANIEL

There once was a man from Babylon named Daniel who was a philosopher for the king who was very close to the queen, too close. Daniel had to flee for his life because the king was going to behead him. Daniel fled to Egypt. While in Egypt he heard that the king had died so he decided to move back to Babylon so he could marry the queen. On the road back to Babylon, Daniel ran into a short old man with a long, flowing white beard and a big white afro with a long multi-colored robe. This old man had a big book in his hands which had lettering that Daniel had never seen before and Daniel knew many languages. Daniel slowly walked over to the old man and looked down upon him and said, "Sir, what is that book about?" The old man looked up and said with a deep voice, "My son, this is the Book of Destiny. Would you like to look at it?" Daniel took the book and slowly opened it with amazement because with the strong lettering, he could not read it. Then he looked at the old man, gave him back the book and asked, "Where are you going?" Then the old man said, "Why I'm going to the festival in the city of Bagdad". (In Babylon) Then Daniel said, "I am going to Bagdad too."

"Would you like to travel together?" Daniel asked. The old man said "Sure, I would like that but only under one condition. That no matter what I do and what you see, you do not question me." Daniel agreed and they left. In those days, there were no motel and hotels. When it became dark, one would just stop at someone's house and ask if they could stay overnight. The first house that they came to was a large mansion. The old man knocked on the door. The servant came and answered the door. The old man asked if they could stay the night. The servant asked the master, the master said yes and they went in. The servant brought them in and showed them the gold and riches of the house and the paintings, sculptures, etc.... Then it became dinnertime, they sat in a room with a long, long table with the master at the other end and Daniel and the old man sat at the other end. The old man doesn't as much as look at them nor did he say one word during the feast. At the end of the dinner, they washed their hands in jeweled encrusted gold finger bowls.

The old man asked the servant to thank the master for his good hospitality. The next day, while on the road, Daniel noticed a big bulge in the old man's pocket. The old man pulled out a gold finger bowl and Daniel got upset and asked the old man, "Why did you steal from that nice man who was so nice to us?" The old man said, "I thought I asked you and you promised not to question anything I did." That same night, they stopped at another mansion and the old man knocked on the door again. The servant answered and they asked the servant if they could stay the night. The servant asked the master then came back and brought them to the barn to sleep. That night, they ate rotten apples and drank stale beer. The old man ate the apples and drank the beer with great enjoyment.

The next morning they woke up and the old man asked the servant to talk with his master. When the master came, the old man said "I would like to give you a token of my appreciation for how good you treated us. Then he reached into his pocket and gave the man the finger bowl. It was the GOLD finger bowl. The master was lost for words. Before he could say anything, they turned and left.

Daniel turned to the old man and asked "Why did you give that old man who treated us so poorly that gold finger bowl?" The old man said, "I thought you weren't going to ask any questions?" That same night, they stopped at another house which was owned by a philosopher who had already heard of Daniel. They went into the house, sat at the table and discussed philosophy and the things they have gone through with the Queen and the city of Babylon. The old man interrupted and said, "You have been very kind but Daniel and I have to get up early in the morning and be on our way." Then the philosopher reached into his pocket and gave them some gold and said, "I see you have nothing, so please take this gold, maybe it will help you." The next morning they got up to leave.

The old man then turned to Daniel and said, "I must repay this man for being so kind to us." He then took a torch and lit the house on fire. Daniel then tried to put the fire out but the old man pulled him away. Daniel screamed, "Hey man, why did you do this? He treated us so well." The old man said, "You promised not to ask any questions." Then they went on their way.

That same afternoon they stopped at the house of a crippled woman for lunch. While they sat and ate she asked them about where they were going. The old man said they were going to Bagdad for the festival. She said, "Why don't you take my nephew with you to show the way because there is abridge that is very, very dangerous to cross on the way. My nephew can show you the way across the bridge." They thanked her and went on their way. While on their way, they came to the bridge. They almost made it across the bridge. The old man then stops and says to the kid, "I have to show my appreciation for your kindness to us. Then takes the boy and throws the boy into the river and the boy drowns."

Now Daniel went crazy. "How could you do that? He takes care of the old lady. That's it. I'm not going any further with you." Daniel is now screaming and yelling. While he was yelling, he noticed the old grey man getting younger and younger looking. Then he sprouted some wings, and then Daniel steps back in great shock with no more words to say. The once old man said, "I am the angel of Jared." Daniel said to him, "If you are an angel, why did you do all that stuff that you did?" The angel Jared said, "MAN CANNOT SEE THE TRUTH BEHIND THE EVENTS OF HIS LIFE."

He said, for example, "The first house we stopped at I stole that gold finger bowl because the master of the house was so arrogant. It was beneath him to even speak to us. We weren't even worthy to have him speak to us. He had his servant show us all his rich things and wealth. I stole the bowl from him because maybe next time, he would treat his guest with more consideration and kindness. Maybe the next guest won't steal from him."

I gave the bowl to the next man because maybe the next time he won't treat his guest so poorly and won't make him sleep in the barn eating rotten apples and drinking stale beer.

And for your friend, the philosopher, he is now the richest man
in babylon. There was a great treasure buried under his house
wich he would have never found unless i burned his house down,
then daniel said ok, ok what about the boy in the river?
Who is going to take care of his aunt?
What did you kill the boy for?
Then the angel said, in two years he would have killed the
queen, then daniel said couldent you have warned the boy?
Couldent we have said somthing to him?
Then the angel said but if i let him live, he would have killed
his aunt, his wife his kids and himself, then he asked the angel
why do things have to be like this, the way they are on earth?
The angel said, god has created many worlds in other worlds, the
same events turn out differently in this would, this was the way
things were ment to be, all of life is a test of rewards and punishment.
But in every event, there is always a lesson to learn, yet all
things work together for the good to those that love the
lord and who are called according to his purpose.

FINAL CALL FOR THE ROLLER COASTER RIDE

Come take a ride with me
Let your mind travel
As we all take a ride on the downside
To the bottom of the barrel
You got that girl? Boy?
Man, I aint' tryin' ride with no boy
Unless we all hang out
Driving down the fast lane
On the main line
Can we speed
And I fly like a boat
I like to be on
But I love to get off
Take a ride on the passenger side
While I cruise
We have nothing to lose
I'm the boss
Nobody tells me nothing
I'm the captain of this ship
L-S-D-T-H-C, O-D
Who was the undertaker
Wow, what a nice hearse
It's a Cadillac
Last slow ride
You on the inside
Last stop
The graveyard
Final call
For the roller coaster ride.

WHY YOU WANT TO BE A DRUG DEALER?

It is exceptional for exchanges to be made
As long as the proper person exclaims
And the exemplification is all about getting paid
And we are the exhibit

We fly no planes, we own no trains
The white house must have their hand in the kettle
Their finger on metal
As cocaine and heroine fills the rich man's pockets
An underground supermarket
Exceeding super numbers for the superior
Or shall I say inferior
And as we know the liar is the supplier we all support
When you find yourself alone, talking into the microphone
Pleading your case in superior court
Why you want to be a drug dealer?

Nameless and shameless is the contact man
It's even hard for the National Guard to understand
He supplies the jail with those who fail
For justice or just on the richer scale
The building always overflows
A minor setback, a political attack
On those who are blind, on those who don't know
We fly no planes or own no trains
So where does all this money go?

Continued

205

Inner city lover, living in the gutter
Ride the main line one more time
Got your own works today
Sleeping sickness no last wish
Your final resting place is where you lay.

The government lies and tries to close its eyes
But we all know the truth
And the truth has set us free
We stop and stare and know it's not fair
For the things we hold in our memory.

Misrepresentation has brainwashed the nation
And those with pigmentation stereotype
They want us to believe we are enemies
We deal drugs on the street and for that street we fight
When a young life is taken a hole in the neighborhood is shaken
And prisons are full of those who believe we should unite
Off with your head is what the judge said
And you still believe that dealing drugs is alright.

Can't you see the strategy?
The plans that have been made to keep us oppressed
We fly no planes or own no trains
And still we settle for less
The player gets played
And who gets paid
The state, the government and the IRS
How can you be the shit smoking that cigarette
When all you end up with
Is time and hope to pass a GED test.

Continued

We fly no planes or own no trains
But they call us the drug trafficker of the US
Drugs come from another land into your hand
Then to the witness stand while you confess.

A mother shun me
Said her kids are hungry
She got no money cause she blew her check
She got evicted, her home is restricted
They got no place to go, no change of clothes
And in that same breath she sadly confessed
She wanted more dope to feed her nose.

I saw a little boy jumping for joy
He said when he got older he wanted to go live with his daddy
But daddy is in jail
Mommy is never home and he's always alone
Did you hear from daddy?
I've been checking the mail.

I wish my mother was alive
She won't believe her eyes
To see her son living this way
Because when she was around
I was drugged down
Getting high every day
It is exceptional for changes to be made
As long as the proper person exclaims
And the exemplification is about getting paid
For the cash money big wheeler
We fly no planes or own no trains
So why do you want to be a drug dealer?

DO YOU KNOW WHO WE ARE?

Black man
Who are you?
African American man
Who are you?
Jamaican, African, Ethiopian
No one wants to be an African American
America, America, the land of the rich
The land of the free
We come to this land for opportunity
The melting pot is hot for the African American
Yes, that's what they call me
In this land of opportunity
Some call me nigger, some call me black
Am I home? Is this my land? Where am I at?
Who am I? Whose blood is running through my vains?
How did I get here? Where am I gong?
What is my real name?
Black, African American, Negro, Colored
A culture with many names
Do you know who we are?

LORD FIX ME

God's infinite power is without limit

God spoke the word into existence. In the beginning he created the heavens and the earth. He created light and darkness, then separated the two, called the light 'day' and the darkness he called 'night'.

God created the "firmament" and divided the waters; he spoke vegetation into existence; created the birds, the bees, the trees, fruit and seed.

God created the stars in heaven and the galaxies; he spoke into existence, all the creatures in the waters and on earth, then he stepped back, took a look, and saw *that it was good*.

He took dirt from the ground, blew his breath of life into it and created man. He gave man dominion over all living things, in the water and on earth. He created man in his own image, a "master at work".

Then God reached inside of man, pulled out a rib and created woman, blessed them and said, "Be fruitful and multiply". Then he stepped back, took a look and said, "Behold, *it is good*". Once again the master was at work.

The creator of time and everlasting, the same God who came from everlasting into our time, became what he created; came from the womb of a woman, put on the flesh of man, took the sins of the world, 'nailed' them to the stake, 'died' and 'woke Jesus up three days later.'

There is no limit to the power of God. He is a master of creation and he specializes in change. He affects lives in the water and on earth. The greatest creation is mankind and we need to keep our young people in prayer and ask the Lord to give them direction and influence them to do good. May they be reconciled and redeemed and to change them from a weak sinner into a strong saint. Like the song says, a saint is just a sinner who fell down and got back up.

DO NOT JUDGE

In fact most of the time, when we judge others, we misjudge them, in our own foolish thoughts. The Book of Matthew tells of the good news that the long awaited Messiah had come to save the people. Matthew is one of the twelve disciples and is believed to be the author of this book and it is believed to have been written about 70 A.D. In this book, Matthew presents Christ as the Great Teacher who helps us understand God's Law and tells us about the Kingdom of God and what it is. In this book we find a sermon that Jesus gave on a mountainside which is called the Sermon on the MT. Matthew 5:1-7:27. In this book we find another teaching of Jesus, we call this teaching The Beatitudes. Let's read Matthew 5: 1-2, Looking at Chapter 5 to Chapter 7: Jesus teaches about attitudes, salt and light, murder, adultery, divorce, oaths, an eye for an eye, loving your enemies. Let me repeat that one, "Loving Your Enemies" and Giving to the Needy, all of this is just in Chapter 5. Chapter 6, he teaches about prayer, fasting, treasures in Heaven. Not to worry, he begins Chapter 7 with "Judging Others". The Beatitudes, what an attitude to be in, judging others or misjudging others. Let's focus on Matthew 7:1-5, in verses one through four, it's talking about those times when you look at another brother or sister and say things like, "she's fake" or "he's not a real Christian", or "I heard him say a bad word the other day", "Girl, didn't she wear that same dress last week?" "She is so cheap, they only put five dollars in the plate last week. Now I know they could have given more to the church." Or, "Their kids are so bad." You know what I am talking about, I am talking about judging others!!! It's bad enough that we have the world judging and misjudging the church. Judgment is going to begin in the House of God, yet we sit around and misjudge each other, putting each other down. IT'S UNHOLY, IT'S UNGODLY, Read Hebrew 3:8-16.

ONE STEP FORWARD
AND
TWO STEPS BACKWARD

I live in a world of selfishness and hate where greed is
guaranteed to dominate
I take one step forward and two steps back
I wake up in the morning, where am I at
To understand where I'm at,
One has to know to where I've been
Do you understand where I'm coming from?
Did you hear the news?
A man tried to walk in my shoes,
He broke all the rules
And now he h as nothing but the blues
Having everything to lose
My life is a constant struggle
I live day for day
In a world of selfishness and hate
Where nothing comes my way
America, America
The land of the free
Do I have a job?
Man times are hard
I've applied, but no one will hire me
Some look at me strange
They don't believe in change
So they misjudge me
By my criminal record
They call my Cori
America, America
The land of the free
The land of opportunity

Continued

So being the man that I am
I played the hand life dealt to me
Life handed me a lemon
And I made lemonade
And gossip is going around town
People wondering
How does he get paid?
How do I exist?
Well if you really want to know
It goes a little something like this

I got more bills than I got cash
And I'm constantly being judged by my past
Some put me down
And some stereotype
My wrong is wrong, and so is my right
I took the bad that I had
And became a man
I just want to help others
Through my youth program, my youth program
I use to gang bang, sell and use drugs
All my life surrounded by thieves and thugs
I spent most of my life in a jail cell
Improving my life and trying to get well
I've been stabbed, shot at, I even been dead
I've tried many ways to work and get ahead
I take one forward, and two steps back
America, America
Where am I at?
I took the hand life dealt to me
And I tried to help others
Children that are self destructing
And heartbroken mothers
And as poor as I am

Continued

In the land of the rich the home of the free
I'm still able to give something back to my community
So don't judge me by the wrong I've done
Focus on the good that I do
See God is the judge
And believe me he won't misjudge you
When I help one child
That's my job, this is my pay
I feel like a million dollars
When I walk away
In jail I woke up in fear
Today I wake up in prayer
Thanking God for allowing me to be here
For having something to share
To the lost child that's going nowhere
Cause I've been their
And life isn't fair
When your feel that nobody cares
So this is my job and that's what I do
I mentor, I educate, the youth
To respect life's values
So they don't have to go through
What I've gone through
So can I get some support from you?
Or do you put me down
And misjudge me
In this land of the rich
And the home of the free
If you walk in my shoes
Before you plan your attack
You'll take one step forward
And two steps back

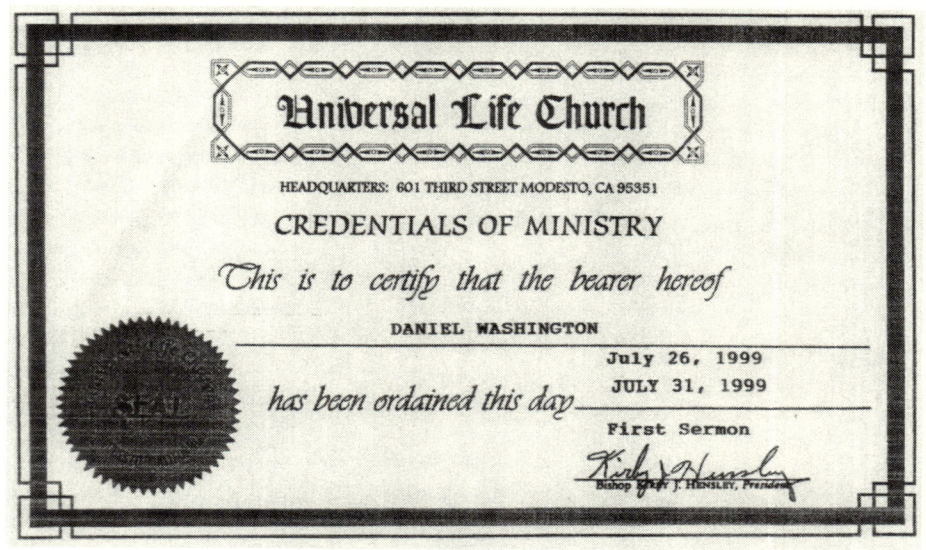

SOUTHEASTERN
CORRECTIONAL CENTER

MASSACHUSETTS

CERTIFICATE OF PARTICIPATION

Daniel J. Washington

has voluntarily participated in Group Psychotherapy for Men Who Wish to Work on Managing Their Anger and Aggression

from **6/20/96** to **3/13/97**

*In recognition of your motivation, contributions and progress
this award is presented*

THIS **17th** DAY OF **November** 19**98**

J. TYLER CARPENTER, PH.D., ABPP
COORDINATOR OF CLINICAL TRAINING

DONNA G. COLLINS
DIRECTOR OF TREATMENT

Attended group therapy in MCI-Concord - 8/8/95 to 12/12/95

215

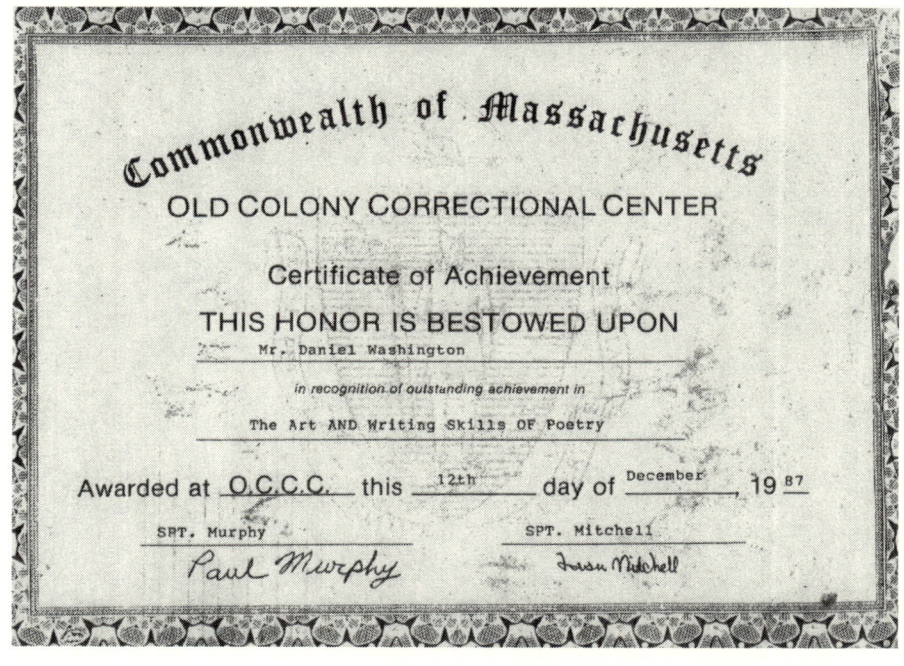

Commonwealth of Massachusetts

OLD COLONY CORRECTIONAL CENTER

Certificate of Achievement

THIS HONOR IS BESTOWED UPON

Mr. Daniel Washington

in recognition of outstanding achievement in

The Art AND Writing Skills OF Poetry

Awarded at O.C.C.C. this 12th day of December, 19 87

SPT. Murphy

Paul Murphy

SPT. Mitchell

Susan Mitchell

216

The **AFRICAN AMERICAN COALITION COMMITTEE**

An inmate organization at M.C.I. Norfolk Prison

On behalf of our membership, as well as other inmate Groups recognizing the outstanding achievements of outstanding men,

PRESENTS TO:

Daniel Washington

ON THIS 8TH DAY OF FEB Y2K

AN AWARD OF APPRECIATION TO EXPRESS OUR GRATITUDE FOR THE SUPPORT YOU HAVE GIVEN US AND OTHERS, AND FOR MAKING LIVES WHEREVER YOU GO BETTER.

SINCERELY,

_____
CHAIRMAN

_____
VICE CHAIRMAN

217

About the Author

I grew up in the project in Brockton, Mass, in Boston Mass in the gutter the ghetto surrounded by drugs pimps whores and hustlers. Our house was a party was the party house after hours card games gambling shooting and stabbings. At a young age I saw more than the average adult. By the age of 14 year old I was addicted to armed robberies, power and control. I've been involved with guns, drugs and violence. At 16 years old I was on probation for 5 to 7 years. At 16.5 I was doing hard time in Walpole State Prison. I grew up in prison, that were I became man. I served a 3 to 5 then 5 to 7 then 6 to 8 then 9 to 12 with a county six month bid to top it off.

I'm 43 years old now and since I been out of prison I married, and I'm living the dream of success. Success to me is no more crime, no more time. I have a wife and my 4 children in my life. She has 8, I have 4, so I father 12 children. I took the hand that life dealt to me and started a youth program called Become Won inc. Which stands for Bridging endless community oppression, mentoring educating and winning our neighborhoods. I run this with my wife, and children. We mentor the youth to stay away from gangs, drugs, and violence

I give poetry workshops. My wife writes plays and we even go into school classrooms speaking to the youth. I'm a strong believer in change. I believe if we can reach just one and teach just one, that we can make a positive change in our community.

So I took the hand that life dealt to me and played it to my best ability. My only prayer is that this book a help change a young life and give some one a better outlook on life.

I don't want no one to experience the pain and sufferings that I have experienced in and out of prison. So please read this book and pass it on.

Proceeds from this book will be used to continue to help us help our youth. By buying this book, you will be making your contribution to help save some lives giving sight to the blind, and insight to those who are still living in darkness.

We can make a better life for our young ones.

That is what I was…This is who I became.

Printed in the United States
217627BV00001B/35/P